The Stones that the Builders Rejected

The Stones
that the
Builders
Rejected

The Development
of Ethical
Leadership
from the Black
Church Tradition

Edited by
Walter Earl Fluker

TRINITY PRESS INTERNATIONAL
Harrisburg, Pennsylvania

Trinity Press International, P.O. Box 1321, Harrisburg, PA 17105
Trinity Press International is a division of the Morehouse Group

Library of Congress Cataloging-in-Publication Data
The stones that the builders rejected : the development of ethical
   leadership from the Black church tradition / edited and with an
   introduction by Walter Earl Fluker.
       p.   cm.
   Includes bibliographical references.
   ISBN 1–56338–235–0
   1. Afro-Americans – Religion. 2. Leadership – Religious aspects.
   3. Leadership – Moral and ethical aspects – United States.
   I. Fluker, Walter Earl, 1951– .
   BR563.N4S79 1998
   277.3'0829'08996073 – dc21   97–49922

Printed in the United States of America

98   99   00   01   02   10   9   8   7   6   5   4   3   2   1

In memory of
Samuel DeWitt Proctor
(1921–1997)

Here stands the mean uncomely stone,
'Tis very cheap in price!
The more it is despised by fools,
The more loved by the wise.
— ARNALDUS DE VILLANOVA

Come to him, that living stone, rejected by men but in God's sight chosen and precious; and like living stones be yourselves built into a spiritual house, to be a holy priesthood, to offer spiritual sacrifices acceptable to God through Jesus Christ. For it stands in scripture:

"Behold, I am laying in Zion a stone, a cornerstone chosen and precious, and he who believes in him will not be put to shame."

To you therefore who believe, he is precious, but for those who do not believe,

"The very stone which the builders rejected has become the head of the corner,"

and,

"A stone that will make men stumble, a rock that will make them fall";

for they stumble because they disobey the word, as they were destined to do. But you are a chosen race, a royal priesthood, a holy nation, God's own people, that you may declare the wonderful deeds of him who called you out of darkness into his marvelous light. Once you were no people but now you are God's people; once you had not received mercy but now you have received mercy.

I PETER 2:4–10

Contents

Acknowledgments

This book would have been impossible without the generous support of the W. K. Kellogg Foundation, which provided a four year grant (1993–1997) for the establishment of The National Resource Center for the Development of Ethical Leadership from the Black Church Tradition at Colgate Rochester Divinity School/Bexley Hall/Crozer Theological Seminary in Rochester, New York. My gratitude for the support of Ms. Freddye Webb-Petett, Director, The Kellogg International Leadership Program, and her able executive secretary, Ms. Sue Teeters, is immeasurable. Special thanks are also extended to The Louisville Institute and Dr. James Lewis for a grant to support a semester's leave to begin this writing project and others yet in process. The staff of the National Resource Center from 1993–1997, Reverend Natalie Alford, Reverend Joseph Crockett, Dr. Donald Matthews, Mrs. Scheryll Murray, Dr. Richard Douglass, Dr. Ingrid Overacker, Reverend Valeria Lassiter, Mrs. Nancy Merritt, Ms. Joan Bellitera, and Dr. Brad Gundlach, deserve special acknowledgment for their efforts in the development and successful completion of the project. The faculty, staff, and students at Colgate Rochester Divinity School provided the institutional resources and the lively intellectual environment for the work of the project. Dr. Lewis King, Ms. Mary Frances Winters, Ms. Wyoma Best, Mr. Mutui Fabgayi, Reverend Beatrice Paul Harris, and Dr. Marcus Robinson served as advisors and special staff in the various research and programmatic initiatives of the National Resource Center. Ms. Tyra L. Seldon worked closely with the editor in the compilation and editing of the manuscript.

Finally, this book is dedicated to the memory of our beloved mentor and friend, Dr. Samuel DeWitt Proctor, pastor, preacher, theologian, statesman, educator — and a "stone, chosen and precious," in the building of a new world.

Contributors

Carolyn C. Denard is Associate Professor of English, Georgia State University, Atlanta.

Michael Eric Dyson is Senior Research Scholar, Institute for Research in African-American Studies, Columbia University, New York.

Walter Earl Fluker is Executive Director of the Leadership Center, Morehouse College, Atlanta.

Cheryl Townsend Gilkes is John D. and Catherine T. MacArthur Associate Professor of African-American Studies and Sociology and Director of African-American Studies, Colby College, Waterville, Maine.

Clarice J. Martin is Jean Picker Associate Professor of Philosophy and Religion, Department of Philosophy and Religion, Colgate University, Hamilton, New York.

Peter J. Paris is Elmer G. Homrighausen Professor of Christian Social Ethics and Liaison with Princeton University's Afro-American Studies Program, Princeton Theological Seminary, Princeton, New Jersey.

Marcia Y. Riggs is Associate Professor of Christian Ethics, Columbia Theological Seminary, Decatur, Georgia.

1

Introduction

The Failure of Ethical Leadership and the Challenge of Hope

WALTER EARL FLUKER

The judgment of God appears again and again in the process of history, dramatized by the rise and fall of peoples who have neglected to build their civilizations towards the higher ends of ethical responsibility . . . the diabolical character of the enterprise itself destroys the vehicle so that finally the energies are scattered and dissipated.[1]

The Challenge of Leadership and the Spirit of Meanness

There is a crisis in leadership that reaches across the social, religious, economic, and political spectrum and touches every facet of our lives. The moral failures at the highest levels of government and the accompanying spirit of meanness play out in the violence of inept and corrupt public policy and on the streets of our nation's inner cities.[2] The prescriptions for the cure of this spiritual malady are many and varied: new age spirituality, managerial and therapeutic discourses, quick-fix religious conversions, and a deluge of tall, good-looking, chiseled, athletic heroes who assure us that the right body weight and focused mental energies will earn us a place in the pantheon of the get-rich-through-your-own-will-to-achieve crowd. Underneath the maddening calls to prosperity via profit-maximizing individualism is a deeper and more fundamental problem that I am calling "the failure of ethical leadership."

The problem of ethical leadership is the failure of public leaders to resolve America's long history of shame and to address what constitutes the human need for love, hope, and a sense of community.[3] The recent resignations of senior legislators, the outcries for democratic renewal, and the call for a politics of meaning are responses to the manifestations of the degeneration of spiritual and ethical foundations of American civil society.[4] This failure rests on the struggle for recognition (*megalothymia*) — the inordinate need to be honored and respected, the need to stand out as symbol of prowess and power, to demand by height what one fails to achieve by depth, to wrest from the other what one thinks is absent in oneself, and to find security in the obsequiousness and submission of the other.[5]

The problem of modern liberal democracy is the problem of this inordinate need for recognition. This sickness of the soul is wrought by a sensate culture that has inverted on itself — it is madness, the insatiable passion for domination of the other. The rise in racially motivated and domestic violence, child abuse, white militia movements, and violent counter-culture discourses among youth are examples of this phenomenon. At the heart of this problem at the end of this century is the licentious spread of capital and a post-industrial market-stimulated morality; and the ones most severely impacted are the young and poor of our society.

At first glance, such an ethic of recognition seems insane. Why would one assume that his or her liberty is based on the bondage of the other? What sense does it make to rape and pillage for the sake of seeing the enemy tremble? There is something, nonetheless, in human beings that thrives on this sinister need. The nineteenth-century South African writer, Olive Schreiner, says that once she dreamed that God took her soul to hell. Upon arrival she was astounded by its beauty and exclaimed, "I like this place." And God said, "Really!" As she proceeded further she noticed beautiful women everywhere, long flowing robes draped upon their graceful bodies, tasting fruit from the trees. She noticed, however, that they never ate the fruit, but only touched it softly with their mouths and left it hanging on the tree. She asked God why they were only touching the fruit with their mouths but not eating it. God replied that they were really poisoning the fruit. She said to God, "Why are they doing that?" God said, "That another may not eat." She said, "But if they poison all then none dare eat; what do they gain?" God said, "Nothing." She said, "Are they not afraid they themselves may bite where another has bitten?" God said, "They are afraid. In hell, all [people] are afraid."

She went a little further and noticed a group of men busily at work. She said, "I should like to go and work with them. Hell must be a very fruitful place, the grass is so green." God said, "Nothing grows in the garden they are making." She examined the workers more carefully and noticed they were working among the bushes digging holes but setting nothing in them; and when they were a way off they would hide in the bushes watching. She noticed that as each walked he set his foot down carefully looking where he stepped. She said to God, "What are they doing?" God said, "Making pitfalls into which their fellows will fall." "Why do they do it?" she asked. God replied, "Because each thinks that when his brother falls he will rise." She said, "How will he rise?" God answered, "He will not rise." And she saw their eyes gleam from behind the bushes. "Are these men sane?" she asked. God answered, "They are not sane; there is no sane person in hell."[6]

The arrogance and insanity of much of America's top leadership are due to the failure to resolve what Mircae Eliade called, "the terror of history."[7] As a nation, we have unfinished business to take care of with the raped of the world; and we will not have peace and our children will not enjoy true prosperity until our incomplete story is resolved. Malidoma Patrice Somé has written that the great need in Western civilization is the need for "ritualized grief." We have not mourned our dead nor paid penance for our complicity in what James Baldwin called, "the white great lie." The Great Lie of modernity, of Machine Culture, is that there is no real past — only Progress, the forward, future-fixated movement of Western individualism that destroys all connections with the past. Somé writes,

> Modernism means *unemotionalism*, or that which owes emotion to the world. It also means loss of memory of the way of acting that encompasses both the body and the soul. To cleanse the modern world from its unresolved problems of the soul, there ought not to be a Memorial Day but a massive funeral day when everyone is expected to shed tears for the titanic loss wrecked by Progress on people's souls.[8]

Clearly, this search for *soul* is exemplified in the national crisis of leadership. Political scandals, renegade corporate takeovers, banking scams, urban decay, educational policies that place the nation at risk, and violence have become the watchwords of our frightened and confused culture. But the long litany of ills that beset our society is only symptomatic of a deeper problem. America, indeed, is in search of its soul — but the harrowing and nagging specter that hovers over our beleaguered and troubled nation is the loss of memory and the accompanying paralysis of hope. Reinhold Niebuhr once said that America is like a young man suffering from premature senility. Niebuhr felt that in its youthful arrogance and strength, America had forgotten the larger question of its raison d'être.

Amidst the violence, abandonment, fear, and pain that beset our society, it has become increasingly difficult to speak about, even more so to hope in, the meaning of America. The deeper, unanswered question, however, has to do with what constitutes a compassionate and just society. Is there ever a basis, historical or otherwise, for believing in this impossible possibility? Dare we be so naive as to believe that it is possible to hope for a society that is characterized by compassion? I believe we have no choice. To hope is to leave open the possibility, no matter how remote, that we might on these shores and in this world remember what it means to be human — and to strive to make that hope of a beloved community real. But to hope also means to remember. Hope without memory is spurious at best, for hope is riveted in history.

The error that plagues the modernist project, exemplified most dramatically in European colonization, is the elusive ideal of progress that issues forth in a superficial optimism. Christopher Lasch, in *The True and Only Heaven*, suggests that this "optimism" feeds on a nostalgia in which the European memory of collective innocence supersedes and erases the boundaries of history. Hope, on the other hand, according to Lasch, is the product of garnered faith in the potential goodness of life. This hope is not sentimental, does not feed on fictitious innocence, but acknowledges the limitations of history. "Hope," he writes, "does not demand a belief in progress. It demands a belief in justice: a conviction that the wicked will suffer, that wrongs will be made right, that the underlying order of things is not flouted with impunity. . . . "

> Hope implies a deep-seated trust in life that appears absurd to those who lack it. It rests on confidence not so much in the future as in the past. It derives from early memories — no doubt distorted, overlaid with later memories, and thus not wholly reliable as a guide to any factual reconstruction of past events — in which the experience of order and contentment was so intense that subsequent disillusionments cannot dislodge it. Such experience leaves as a residue the unshakable conviction, not that the past was better than the present, but that trust is never completely misplaced, even though it is never completely justified either and therefore destined inevitably to disappointments.[9]

Lasch suggests that great Americans like Reinhold Niebuhr and Martin Luther King Jr. are exemplars of this understanding of hope. These observations are helpful, but they do not get to the grain of the problem, that is, to the intensity of the social evil that masquerades under the unscrupulous, romantic banner of the American dream of progress and the social practices that conspire against those who have no voice. Both Niebuhr and the early King underestimated the radical entrenchment of race in our society and the place of memory in this vicious occnario of conquest and exploitation that predates Columbus's voyage to the New World.

What is America? Is it the failed chronicle of history makers credited with the founding of a nation-state — Washington, Adams, Hamilton, Jefferson, and others — the great white men of the American time line leading to Ronald Reagan? Or are the true history makers the marginalized "who stand outside the time line and every headline"? Does America go on forever?[10] What is the *meaning* of America? If we hear only from the great white men, then America means certain ways of living in the world, but if we could hear from the voices of the marginalized, then America might mean something quite different. The poet Langston Hughes speaks for these voices when he writes, "America never was America to me."[11]

Entangled in the mythology of progress is the fraudulent premise that the founders of this nation intended a society that has compassion for all. Part of the reckoning that must take place in the unraveling of this shroud of innocence is to come to grips with our history — the underside of our story, the story of a people as diverse as the world, yet bound by an ethic of exclusiveness and individualism.

Who, Now, Will Shape the Meaning of America?

In 1981, in the John Courtney Murray Lecture delivered at New York's prestigious Harvard Club, Richard John Neuhaus raised the provocative and timely question, "Who, Now, Will Shape the Meaning of America?"[12] Neuhaus's brief commentary was a precursor to a growing literature on the resurgence of religious discourse in the public domain. It was also a prophetic signal of the decline of triumphant secularity and the rise of a post-secular culture. The role of religion in the shaping of values and public policy has reached an increasing number of publics that extend beyond the conservative/liberal theological stopgap that has historically defined the debate.[13] A stream of public conversations that incorporate therapeutic and managerial discourses has found audiences beyond the traditional academic and ecclesiastical institutions that have long dominated the contest. New counter-culture movements are among the many competitors who compete for voice and place on a rapidly changing playing field.[14] Yet, with few exceptions, the contestants of choice for reshaping the American future do not include the voices of historically marginalized religious communities.[15] Neuhaus, for instance, suggested Catholics, Lutherans, and evangelicals as viable candidates for what sociologist Wilfredo Pareto labeled, "the circulation of elites." Neuhaus made passing references to Martin Luther King Jr.

and the role of religion in the modern civil rights movement, but did not include the many other voices that made King's sonorous baritone possible. His recommendations and those of others reveal the historical dilemma of African Americans and other historically oppressed groups who have been relegated to the "outer regions of darkness," the places and spaces where the exercise of power in articulating a vision for America has been dubbed "illegitimate."[16]

The tendency of public intellectuals to ignore the historical embodiment of power in the discursive practices of the culture makers is a daunting concern for those who speak from behind the veil. Arthur M. Schlesinger Jr., for example, has described the current situation as "the disuniting of America." His reflections on a multicultural society warn of what he perceives as a threat to national identity and cherished customs:

> Instead of a transformative nation with an identity of its own, America increasingly sees itself as preservative of old identities. Instead of a nation composed of individuals making their own free choices, America increasingly sees itself as composed of groups more or less indelible in their ethnic character. The national ideal had once been e pluribus unum. Are we now to belittle unum and glorify pluribus? Will the center hold? Or will the melting pot yield to the Tower of Babel?[17]

Who, now, will shape the meaning, better, the soul of America? While the "Babel myth" is highly appropriate to speak to the incommensurability of moral languages in our culture, I would like to expand the metaphor, so to speak, to include "the stones that the builders rejected." Perhaps the builders of Babel err not because they try to reach the heavens, but because they fail to pay attention to the other essential materials that go into the construction of such a marvelous project. The old biblical adage that is so much a part of African-American Christian experience says, "The stone that the builders rejected has become head of the corner" (Ps. 118:22). The implication is that "history's absent ones" have much more to say about the nature of moral discourse and the redemption of the soul of America than heretofore acknowledged.[18]

A glaring oversight on the part of nearly all the religious and ethical thinkers involved in the debate over religion's role in shaping the public life is the, at best, cursory attention given to the historically oppressed communities within the national life — in this case, to African-American religious and moral traditions. Throughout American history, the black church has provided the pool of leadership that led to the creation of social institutions and organizations that have prophetically challenged the nation to move toward a "beloved community." Because of the black church's distinctive sociocultural location and long history of producing ethical leaders despite inadequate material and social resources, it is a prime candidate for offering direction for the ongoing debate over religion and public life. Moreover, the black church has played a significant role in shaping the moral languages of this nation, and consequently, can serve as a strategic resource in the formation of ethical leadership for national and international communities.

We cannot critically examine the moral discourse and practices in the American experience without taking seriously the long and arduous history of domination, slavery, Jim Crow, segregation, and its consequences on the psychosocial health of all Americans. It is commonplace to begin discussions such as these by focusing primarily on African Americans as victims of these sordid realities. But it is impossible to talk about the oppression of African Americans as a one-dimensional phenomenon having no relation to the dominant culture and the ways in which that culture perpetuates itself through fear and the concomitant power relations that prevent us from seeing the horrible historical truth that all of us are caught in the web of the spider. These fears and power relations are not imaginary ghosts divorced from the actual circumstances that shape relationships between various racial and cultural groups, but are ever present realities that dictate moral discourse. The error of many moral thinkers is the failure to acknowledge the presence of masses of disinherited and dispossessed groups within the power configurations of this culture. In doing so, they have allowed ideology to dominate their understandings of national community, and their resulting analyses and recommendations are bereft of meaningful and substantive measures that speak to the lifeworlds of those whom Samuel Proctor called "the least, the lost, and the left behind."[19]

Perhaps Jeremiah spoke too soon when he claimed, "In those days they shall no longer say: 'The fathers have eaten sour grapes, and the children's teeth are set on edge.' But everyone shall die for his own sin; each man who eats sour grapes, his teeth shall be set on edge" (Jer. 31:29–30). The grapes of wrath in America are very sour — and the children's teeth are decayed. Cornel West and other critical race theorists continue to warn us that *race matters*. The media are filled with commentaries on the place of race in our world: the bombing of black churches, the Million Man March, the Million Women's March, white militia, the significance of race in political campaigns around the nation, the abject poverty fed by systemic racist practices, the vicious cycle of urban violence that threatens to annihilate an entire generation of poor youth and the superficial debate about who is to blame. Who carries the weight of the guilt associated with the failed Tower of Babel in America? *Who is responsible?* Who, now, will shape the soul of America for our children and the children of the world?

It is an easy trick of rationalization to place all the blame on those outside of *us*. The racism that afflicts this country is deeply ingrained in the very soul of the nation — no one escapes. Of course, those situated in the core of our inner cities suffer the most because of poverty, miseducation, and relegation to the margins of the culture, but the untold story is that those who are most victimized are the ones who may hold the secret to the cure for the malady of race. White-funded and white-controlled think tanks offer quantitative studies about the statistical configuration of the problem of race, but the qualitative, spiritual mindscape of those who live daily with the intense effects of race know well that number-crunching offers no real answer. A descriptive analysis is helpful in ascertaining the broad contours and social topography of race, but the underlying discourse that reaches into the souls of the left-out raises a more profound question regarding the antidote for the disease. If we are to find meaning in the struggle to achieve and conform to an authentic identity as a nation, then those who know best what it means to eat sour grapes are the ones who stand in candidacy for being a remedy.

African-American leadership is not exempt from the crisis of spirit that threatens American civil society. Recent revelations of fiscal improprieties and political manipulation in the National Baptist Convention, USA, Inc., the largest of all Black denominations, speak volumes to the issues at stake for all Americans.[20] Moreover, the failure of black leadership articulated by Harold Cruse in *The Crisis of the Negro Intellectual* and the longstanding historical divide between integrationism and black nationalist ideologies still persist. Cruse warned in 1967 that "Every aspect of America's national morality is predicated on a materialistic ethos." He continued, "With no traditional love for the land he adopted, the American has remained to this day a stranger in the land of his birth: ill-at-ease with his power, uncertain about his nationality, an extroverted pragmatist for whom every exposure of the social immorality of his inner life becomes a scandal."[21] Cruse's prophetic denunciation of a spurious integrationist strategy for African Americans was also a statement about the ways in which the underlying discourse of the American moral ideal of democracy has fastened itself to an entrepreneurial ethic that undermines the prospects for racial harmony. At stake in Cruse's cultural analysis is far more than the question of integration versus black nationalism, but the spiritual and moral character of a nation. His treatise served as a critique of the national life as much as of the cultural situation of African Americans. The consequence of the failure to heed Cruse's warning has been the entrapment of African-American leadership in a type of double jeopardy. On one side the entrapment is in what Kevin Gaines labels a "culture of dissemblance," in which "desperation, ambition, and the imperatives of survival produce an ostensibly positive black identity in simplistic, reductive terms that replicate the racist and sexist cultural codes of the oppressive society."[22] On the other side is the inability of black leadership to identify with the critical masses of marginalized African Americans, especially women and youth.[23]

The critical need for African-American leadership at this impasse is a fresh approach to the overwhelming needs of class divisions within its own ranks and to move beyond the unresolved debate between progressive and neoconservative ideologues at the national level on the *politics of race*.[24] While the analyses of the problem of race vary, depending upon ideological commitments, nearly all involved in the ongoing debate agree that the answers to this unresolved dilemma will mark the future of generations of young men and women of every racial and ethnic configuration. An implicit agreement among these interlocutors is that an important dimension of the solution to the malady is spiritual and ethical, and that beyond political, economic, and social remedies there must be an awakening of the masses who provide a new cadre of leadership for the national community.

The call for a new kind of moral leadership emanating from the grassroots is not a new phenomenon in American society, but what is refreshing and potentially creative is the sensitivity to the interrelated necessities of personal and social transformation. A significant element of this new kind of moral leadership is the emphasis on transformation that requires a return to memory as a basis for hope without romanticizing and trivializing the arduous paths that must be tread in order to translate this memory into praxis. The call for a *politics of conversion* presupposes the nexus of memory and hope. African-American leadership cannot begin this spiritual process until there is a willingness to return to its religiocultural roots of sacrifice and service. This return to a sane place will require a radical deconstruction of self in the midst of a multiplicity of forces that stand guard against African Americans' entry into a new future.[25] It is my hope that this volume will make a small contribution towards the rebuilding of the foundations of that new future.

The Development of Ethical Leadership
from the Black Church Tradition

The operative assumption in this volume is that the black church tradition has played a significant role in shaping the moral languages of
this nation, and consequently, can serve as a strategic resource in the
formation of ethical leaders for national and international communities.

The phrase "black church tradition" is used advisedly in this context.
First, this designation is distinct from "the African-American church
tradition" because it encompasses a variety of highly syncretistic religious survivals and retentions from traditional African belief systems
and Christian culture that are more properly referred to under the
canopy of "The Black Church."[26] The black church tradition, at its best,
is an argument about the meaning and destiny of American democratic
dogma;[27] and it finds creative affinity with what James M. Washington
called "the American dissenting tradition," represented most notably
by Martin Luther King Jr. This tradition, according to Washington,
included abolitionists and many other varieties of social reformers.

> Many Americans do not understand or have forgotten how in-
> debted we are to the stubborn tradition of loyal opposition in
> American history. The opposition's determination to put righ-
> teousness, conscience, and morality before social and political
> expediency helped to shape some of our most fundamental values
> and institutions.[28]

Second, the black church tradition is not monolithic, but spans a
broad spectrum of denominational, theological, political, and cultural
diversity.[29] The prophetic strand of the black church tradition referred
to here represents a long stream of tradition in the African-American
community in which *liberation* and *integration* are inextricably linked.
Theologically, Martin Luther King Jr. labeled this quest as the "search
for the beloved community," and Howard Thurman, "the search for
common ground." Lawrence Jones contends that "ever since blacks
have been in America, they have been in search of the 'beloved community,'" a community that is grounded in an unshakable confidence in
a theology of history.[30] The approaches of representatives of this particular strand of the black church tradition to the problem of community
in American society clearly constitute an analysis of the broader problematic of religion, race, and culture. The "thick moral argument" — to
use Michael Walzer's phrase — represented by this tradition can make a
significant contribution to a national community in search of a soul.[31]

The definition of leadership used here borrows from the cognitive approach represented by Howard Gardner. "A leader," according to Gardner, "is an individual (or, rarely, a set of individuals) who significantly affects the thoughts, feelings, and/or behaviors of a significant number of individuals."[32] The central defining motif of leaders, in this perspective, is the place to which they ascribe their authority to story or narrative. Just as leaders are able to articulate stories that shape shared identities and socially constructed realities, leaders are also *storied creatures*.[33] Ethical leaders are both tellers of stories that aspire to truth and the embodiment of the stories that fund ethical insight. Ethical leadership, therefore, refers to the critical appropriation and embodiment of moral traditions that have historically shaped the character and shared meanings of a people (an *ethos*). Ethical leadership does not emerge from an historical vacuum, but arises from the lifeworlds of particular traditions and speaks authoritatively and acts responsibly with the aim of serving the collective good. Ethical leaders are individuals whose characters have been shaped by the wisdom, habits, and practices of particular traditions, often more than one, yet who tend to be identified with a particular ethos and cultural narrative. This understanding of ethical leadership, therefore, is to be differentiated from the popular label, "moral leadership." Ethical leadership refers to "the process of morality to the degree that leaders engage with followers on the basis of *shared motives and values and goals*."[34] While this definition is helpful as a theoretical and heuristic instrument in public policy and values, the perspective articulated here emphasizes the moral development of leaders within communities[35] and their distinctive role as bearers of the stories of their respective traditions. And it is in their remembering, retelling and reliving of these stories and other stories that the possibility of prophetic and creative discourse emerges. Equally critical to goal-oriented leadership is the place of context and followers.[36] Much of the literature on leadership studies is devoted primarily to the development of the leader as a solitary individual, which mirrors the quagmire of utilitarian moral thought that has stymied creativity and fallen prey to the nefarious "bottom line" of Western consumerist culture.[37] More sophisticated approaches challenge the "value-free" presuppositions inherent in definitions of leadership based on prominence, authority, and influence and argue for adaptive, relational, and interactive models of leadership.[38]

A singularly important characteristic of ethical leadership from the black church tradition is the prominence of what I am calling "prophetic narrativity": the call to remember, retell, and relive stories that fund the development of character, civility, and a sense of community. The great ethical leaders from this tradition — preachers, postmodern

academics, lawyers, politicians, and community activists — possess
supreme rhetorical skills and improvisational artistry that capture the
distilled wisdom of communal stories that are, at once, invitational and
dynamic. For these leaders, the prophetic core of the story discourse is
embodied in transformative acts of civility funded by moral imagination.
In the language of Thomas McCollough, they raise the ethical question
in public life.

> To state *the ethical question* as "What is my personal relation to
> what I know?" is to relate *knowledge* to its human, historical con-
> text and to assume *responsibility* for knowledge within that setting.
> So stated, the ethical question provides the knot in the thread,
> lacking which the whole social fabric unravels. The moral factor
> in the process is created by those who take responsibility for ac-
> knowledging it as binding on them — making them accountable
> to it and thus to others who also hold it.[39]

Central to this narrative discourse is the disclosure of meaning that
provides moral insight from particular lifeworlds that speak to the possibility of a collective vision for the national community. More than
ever, there is a need to return, remember, and recollect the substantive
discourse of this tradition for the myriad issues that confront African-
American life and the nation. The call to retrieve and appropriate these
stories is not a romanticization of a golden and innocent past (as the
authors in this volume will remind us); rather it is the critical examination of human narratives that speak to the anguish and resilience of
a dispossessed and disenfranchised people who dared to hope against
hopelessness and to envision the possibility of a human community.

At the center of discussion among ethicists involved in research
and writing on the black church tradition is the development of critical concepts and methods for a social ethic that takes seriously the
indigenous sources and experiences of African-American peoples. All
claim that historically the black church tradition has been the chief
social locus for the ethical foundations of leadership in the African-
American community. The majority of African-American leadership has
been influenced by its distinctive ethos. Throughout its history, the
black church tradition has provided the pool of leadership that led to
the creation of social institutions and organizations that served its constituency and the larger society. The contemporary issue at stake in
African-American moral traditions, as in the larger society, is the role
of systems (institutions, traditions, practices) and their impact on the
moral development of individuals. Simply stated, individuals are socially
constructed yet, by definition, responsible and accountable for moral

choices within the context of their social histories and stories. Hence the pertinent questions for ethics in this respect are: *What is the role of systems in this narrative perspective, and how might the moral agent develop habits and practices that conspire against unjust systemic practices that promote unhealthy and self-destructive existence?*

The scholars in this volume are responding to critical questions formulated to deepen analysis of the black church tradition and to inquire of the critical sources and methodologies that allow for retrieval and appropriation of the substantive discourse of this powerful yet neglected tradition. *How has the black church tradition prepared its constituencies for roles of ethical leadership in the nation? What are the social sources and functions of moral wisdom that this tradition has imparted to generations of ethical leaders? How is the black church tradition's role perceived within the context of contemporary leaders in African-American life?*

A second set of questions inquires of the sources of the black church tradition that produce leaders with national vision. *What are the distinctive features of the black church tradition that incorporate biblical narrative, civic republicanism, and expressive individuality into a moral language about the meaning and destiny of the national community? What critical methodologies are available to identify and retrieve substantive practices of leadership within this tradition and reinterpret them for the contemporary crisis of leadership within the national community?*

One need not look far in scholarly discussions on the significance of the black church tradition to see how these questions articulate organically with the development of leadership from within black communities, but the larger question is: *What does this tradition's proven track record have to contribute to the crisis of leadership in the national and transnational communities?*

The working hypothesis contained in this collection of essays is that because of its distinctive sociocultural location and long history of producing ethical leadership, despite inadequate material and social resources, the black church tradition is a prime candidate for offering direction for the development of leaders for our national and transnational communities.

The authors in this collection represent a cross-disciplinary approach to the problem of ethical leadership from the black church tradition. They provide critical analyses that raise questions concerning the viability of the black church tradition to engage the salient public policy issues that confront black life and culture, and by implication, national policy. These criticisms include intragroup problems (Riggs), an inability to reach black youth (Dyson), and the lack of sustained and systematic ethical guidance (Paris). Clearly, one of the most pressing concerns that challenges black church life and practice, as the scholars in this edition suggest, is the production of a model of ethical leadership that addresses gender and class orientations within its own ranks.

In the first essay, "Moral Development for African-American Leadership," Peter J. Paris offers a neo-Aristotelian approach. He defines ethics as a "practical science" that demands that moral formation move beyond simple cognitive and behaviorist approaches. Paris argues that "thought and knowledge alone will not and cannot effect necessary transformation"; rather, the act of becoming a moral person requires sacrifice and discomfort within a community that is seeking transformation. Transformation, according Paris, cannot occur outside the community. Although "moral action must be voluntary," the community serves as the catalyst and incubator for moral attitudes, habits, and practices. Without "communal stability and consistent training," transformation cannot occur. Paris's definition of ethics and ethical leadership in the black community provides the framework in which the other authors ground their arguments.

The black women's club movement is one example of a strand of this tradition that provided "communal stability and consistent training" to others within the community. Marcia Riggs examines the black women's club movement in her essay "Living into the Bonds of Justice." Riggs contends that the women who participated in the movement were successful because they created a supportive environment based on three moral principles: renunciation, inclusivity, and responsibility. Thus, these women provided support and moral guidance for one another by "recognizing their commonality, creating understanding, and working with diverse classes of women." Although the black church tradition is the foundation for the movement, Riggs warns that we must be self-critical of a tradition that alienates some of it members and makes no attempt to rectify its own internal problems.

Throughout the nineteenth century, black women, like those who participated in the club movement, were recognized as pillars of strength and moral integrity within their respective communities of discourse and practice. Clarice Martin examines the life of Maria Stewart as a model for ethical leadership. In "Normative Biblical Motifs in African-American Leaders' Moral Discourse," Martin describes Stewart's work as an attempt to bring about "advanced spiritual, moral, familial, and psychosocial health and empowerment within black communities." Stewart's effectiveness as an ethical leader was directly impacted by her moral training in the church, yet Martin, like Riggs, suggests that definitions of leaders and leadership must be addressed before the black church tradition can be reappropriated for the good of all the black community. Martin writes that part of the problem with contemporary definitions of black leadership is that the definition fails to incorporate the leadership styles of black women.

Cheryl Townsend Gilkes examines African-American women's organizational political and cultural history as a practical and theoretical resource for defining and interpreting models of ethical leadership. Gilkes contends that although the church has historically been the core community of moral development for African-American women, they were not limited to leadership positions strictly within the church, but used them as a model for other areas of advocacy and leadership. Gilkes argues that by remaining firmly grounded in the ethical principles instilled in them by the black church, these women were able to survive and overcome obstacles; and that invaluable lessons from their examples can fund ethical insights into moral dilemmas facing contemporary leadership. The lessons to be learned from African-American women's leadership, Gilkes suggests, are: (1) leaders must persist in resistance to disconnection; (2) leaders must recognize the importance of the cultural dimension in defining and shaping ways in which issues of social change are addressed; and (3) leaders must recognize and appreciate the need for "collective discipline." Unfortunately, she adds, the models created by these women are not being reappropriated to address contemporary issues facing the black community that Riggs and Martin indicate in their essays.

Another approach to retrieving and reappropriating sources for developing models for ethical leadership is through the identification and usages of narrative, autobiographical, and historical texts. Carolyn Denard focuses on narratives and literary texts in her essay "Retrieving and Reappropriating the Values of the Black Church through Written Narratives." Denard employs fictional works of black authors as guides for excavating the moral discourse of black communities. Emphasizing the representation of character as a distinct literary and ethical form, Denard identifies a common theme of spiritual connection and communal responsibility throughout the texts.

In both forms of retrieval, literary and historical, there is a conscious effort to be inclusive of the diverse issues that face African Americans, including issues of class and gender. Womanist scholars argue that such an approach has been gravely neglected in contemporary ethical discourse on leadership. Subsequently, ethical leaders previously excluded or ignored bring a rich diversity of stories that enliven and expand the stock of dramatic resources available for the development of models for leadership.

In "Ethical Leadership in Black America: Malcolm X, Urban Youth

Culture, and the Resurgence of Nationalism," Michael Eric Dyson's re-appropriation of Malcolm X as a heroic symbol for today's black youth seeks to address the important discussion of leadership that Martin raises in her essay. Dyson, in step with womanist scholars, calls for critical reassessment of leadership styles and ideals within the black church tradition and African-American moral traditions that negatively impact the lives of followers. Arguably, Malcolm X is not a representa-tive of the black church tradition. His inclusion in this volume serves as a healthy critique of and caution against the temptation to think of black religious traditions in exclusionary terms. Dyson suggests that any attempt at retrieval and reappropriation must take into account the di-verse lifeworlds of African Americans, which include the incorporation of diverse sites of oppression. Sites of oppression are sites of memory that make available strategies for survival and liberation within complex hegemonic institutional practices.

Although all six authors offer distinct methodological approaches for understanding ethical leadership, the emphasis and lesson remain the same: the need to return to the powerful resources of the past as a way of rethinking appropriate forms and styles of leadership at this critical impasse in the lives of African Americans and the nation at large. This is a call to the multifaceted tasks of sacrifice and service, of dismantling the simultaneity of racism and sexism, and of realistically addressing the concerns of America's urban youth. For the authors these are not isolated issues of the African-American community; rather, they are sig-nificant indicators of the problem of the crisis of ethical leadership and of a nation in search of a *soul*.

Notes

1. Howard Thurman, "Judgment and Hope in the Christian Message," *The Christian Way in Race Relations*, ed. William Stuart Nelson (New York: Harper and Brothers, 1948), 230.

2. Nicolaus Mills, *The Triumph of Meanness: America's War Against Its Better Self* (Boston and New York: Houghton Mifflin Company, 1997).

3. Stuart Schneiderman, *Saving Face: America and the Politics of Shame* (New York: Alfred A. Knopf, 1995).

4. Michael Lerner, *The Politics of Meaning: Restoring Hope and Possibility in an Age of Cynicism* (Reading, Mass.: Addison-Wesley, 1996); Jean Bethke Elshtain, *Democracy on Trial* (New York: Basic Books, 1995); Charles Derber, *The Wilding of America: How Greed and Violence Are Eroding Our Nation's Character* (New York: St. Martin's Press, 1996) are among the many social and cultural com-mentaries that point to the problem of the loss of ethical and spiritual integrity

in the contemporary debates surrounding character, civility, and community in American society.

5. Francis Fukuyama, *The End of History and the Last Man* (New York: The Free Press), 141–339.

6. Olive Schreiner, "The Sunlight Lay across My Bed," in *A Track to The Water's Edge*, ed. Howard Thurman (New York: Harper and Row, 1973), 64–66.

7. For an exposition of "the terror of history," see Mircea Eliade, *The Myth of the Eternal Return, or Cosmos and History* (New York: Harper and Row, 1991), 156–57.

8. Malidoma Patrice Somé, *Ritual: Power, Healing, and Community* (Portland, Oreg.: Swan Raven and Company, 1993), 122. Grieving requires "re-memory," to use Toni Morrison's language. It is a return not merely to intellectual excavation of historical data, but is associated with deep emotional energy that is spiritual and emphatic. To participate in grief offers entree into worlds of meaning, into forgotten and dis-membered bodies of experience that lie hidden and invisible to consciousness. In the act of "rememory," access is given to theopoetic discourse, which is the primal language of soul. "Rememory," in Morrison, functions to re-collect, re-assemble, and re-configure individual and collective consciousness into a meaningful and sequential whole through the process of narrativization (Mae G. Henderson, "Toni Morrison's *Beloved*: Re-membering the Body as Historical Text," in *Comparative American Identities: Race, Sex, and Nationality in the Modern Text*, ed. Hortense J. Spillers [New York and London: Routledge, 1991], 71). The significance of rememory in grief is the narrativization of the past, the reclaiming of bodies of disparate and disconnected meaning lodged in the unconscious matrices of the soul. In an interview on her novel, *Beloved*, Morrison states, "There is no place you or I can go, to think about or not think about, to summon the presences of, or recollect the absences of slaves; nothing that reminds us of the ones who made the journey and of those who did not make it. There is no suitable memorial or plaque or wreath or wall or park or skyscraper lobby. There's no 300–foot tower. There is no small bench by the road" ("A Bench by the Road," *The World: Journal of the Unitarian Universalist Association* 3 [January–February 1989]: 4–5, 37–40). In a 1977 interview with Paula Giddings, Morrison explains, "The memory is long beyond the parameters of cognition. I don't want to sound too mystical about it, but I feel like a conduit, I really do. I'm fascinated about what it means to make people remember what I don't even know" (Paula Giddings, "The Triumphant Song of Toni Morrison," *Encore* [12 December 1977]: 26–30, quoted in Carolyn C. Denard, "Toni Morrison," in *Modern American Women Writers* [New York: Scribners, 1991], 317). Morrison's narrative strategy is a "kind of literary archeology" in which she uses imaginative and cultural knowledge to retrieve and reconstruct the past of African Americans. Thus her works are sites of "dangerous memories," small benches by the road, memorials that invoke grief and healing.

9. Christopher Lasch, *The True and Only Heaven: Progress and Its Critics* (New York: W. W. Norton, 1991), 81.

10. Walter Brueggemann, "Blessed Are the History Makers," in *Hope within History* (Atlanta: John Knox Press, 1987), 49ff.

11. Langston Hughes, "Let America Be America Again," in *The Negro Caravan: Writings by the Negro*, ed. Sterling H. Brown, Arthur P. Davis, and Ulysses Lee (New York: Dryden Press, 1941), 370.

12. Richard Neuhaus, "Who, Now, Will Shape the Meaning of America?" in *Moral Issues and Christian Response*, 4th ed., ed. Paul T. Jersild and Dale A. Johnson (New York: Holt, Rinehart and Winston, 1988), 36–44.

13. The list is long and includes a range of scholarly treatments from religious liberals and conservatives, theologians, ethicists, legal scholars, and sociologists: Ronald F. Thiemann, *Religion in Public Life: A Dilemma for Democracy* (Washington, D.C.: Georgetown University Press, 1996); Robert Wuthnow, *The Restructuring of American Religion: Society and Faith Since World War II* (Princeton: Princeton University Press, 1988); Robert Wuthnow, *Sharing the Journey: Support Groups and America's New Quest for Community* (New York: Free Press, 1994); Robert Wuthnow, ed., *I Come Away Stronger: How Small Groups Are Shaping American Religion* (Grand Rapids: Eerdmans, 1994); Robert Wuthnow, *Christianity and Civil Society: The Contemporary Debate* (Valley Forge: Trinity Press International, 1996); Stephen Carter, *The Culture of Disbelief: How American Law and Politics Trivialize Religious Devotion* (Basic Books, 1993); Wade Clark Roof and William McKinney, *American Mainline Religion: Its Shape and Changing Future* (Rutgers University Press, 1987); Michael Cromartie, ed., *Disciples and Democracy: Religious Conservatives and the Future of American Politics* (Washington, D.C.: Ethics and Public Policy Center and Eerdmans, 1994); John A. Coleman, "Under the Cross and the Flag: Reflections on Discipleship and Citizenship in America," *America*, 11 May 1996, 6–14; "Religion and Politics," *America*, 3 August 1996, 3; Gustav Niebuhr, "Public Supports Political Voice for Churches," *New York Times*, 25 June 1996, sec. A, 18; Lydia Saad, "America's Religious Commitment Affirmed," *The Gallup Poll*, January 1996, 21–22; Martin Durham, "The Road To Victory? The American Right and the Clinton Administration," *Parliamentary Affairs*, April 1996, 343–53; Joseph C. Shapiro and Andrea R. Wright, "The Faith Factor: Can Churches Save America?" *U.S. News and World Report*, 9 September 1996, 46–53.

14. For recent books and articles see Deepak Chopra, *The Seven Spiritual Laws of Success: A Practical Guide to the Fulfillment of Your Dreams* (Amber-Allen Publishing and New World Library, 1994); Herbert Benson, *Timeless Healing: The Power and Biology of Belief* (New York: Scribners, 1996); Larry Dossey, *Healing Words: The Power of Prayer and the Practice of Medicine* (San Francisco: HarperSanFrancisco, 1993); Larry Dossey, *Prayer Is Good Medicine: How to Reap the Healing Benefits of Prayer* (San Francisco: HarperSanFrancisco, 1996); Charles Trueheart, "Welcome to the Next Church," *Atlantic Monthly*, August 1996, 37–44, 46–47, 50, 52–54, 56–58; Roger Kamenetz, "In The Beginning There Was a Bible Discussion Group. And Then PBS Came Calling," *New York Times Magazine*, 20 October 1996, 64–66; Eugene Taylor, "Desperately Seeking Spirituality," *Psychology Today*, November–December 1994, 54–68.

15. Harvey Cox, *Fire From Heaven: The Rise of Pentecostal Spirituality and the Reshaping of Religion in the Twenty-first Century* (Reading, Mass.: Addison-Wesley, 1995); Thiemann, *Religion in Public Life*; Coleman, "Under the Cross and the Flag"; Robert Bellah, *The Good Society* (New York: Alfred J. Knopf, 1994) are examples of scholars involved in the debate who recognize the place of black religious traditions in the shaping of values and public policy.

16. "The issue in America between blacks and whites," opines David W. Wills, "has ... most essentially been one of power — its exercise and meaning — not prejudice. It has always been central to the issue of politics as a whole, for it touches on the very way American social reality was constituted — *at the beginning* — and maintained ever since by the exercise of power" (David W. Wills, "Beyond Commonality and Plurality: Persistent Racial Polarity in American Religion and Politics," in *Religion and American Politics: From the Colonial Period to the 1980s* [New York: Oxford University Press, 1990], 202). Although one might object to Wills's use of "prejudice" as being distinct from the issue of power, the thrust of the statement underscores a fundamental presupposition about institutionalized power in the contemporary debate surrounding the meaning and formation of community in America. See also Evelyn Brooks Higginbotham's discussion of "The Black Church as Public Sphere," in *Righteous Discontent: The Women's Movement in the Black Baptist Church 1880–1920* (Cambridge: Harvard University Press, 1993), 7–13.

17. Arthur Schlesinger Jr., *The Disuniting of America: Reflections on a Multi-Cultural Society* (Knoxville: Whittle Direct Books, 1991), 2. For systemic critiques of the incommensurability of moral languages in Western culture, see Alasdair MacIntyre, *After Virtue* (South Bend, Ind.: University of Notre Dame Press, 1984); Robert Bellah et al., *Habits of the Heart: Individualism and Commitment in American Life* (New York: Harper and Row, 1986); Vincent Harding, "Toward a Darkly Radiant Vision of America's Truth," *Crosscurrents* 37, no. 1 (spring 1987); Jeffrey Stout, *Ethics after Babel: The Language of Morals and Their Discontents* (Boston: Beacon Press, 1988), 191–242. See the critique of Stout by Sheila Briggs and Cornel West in *Theology Today* (April 1990).

18. The story of the Tower of Babel is well known. Traditional biblical commentators have tended to treat it as "a mythical or legendary account of the breaking up of the primitive unity of humankind into separate communities, distinguished and isolated by differences of language.... The story reflects ... the impression made on Semitic nomads by the imposing monuments of Babylonian civilization" (John Skinner, *A Critical and Exegetical Commentary on Genesis* [New York: Scribner's Sons, 1910], 223). The story of Babel serves as a prologue, an introduction to the story of Abraham, who represents the new faithfulness required by God in the extension of the human family — a family through which God will correct the damage of Babel and bless the nations of the earth. But there is another interpretation of the story of Babel (see Walter Brueggemann, *Genesis* [Atlanta: John Knox Press, 1982], 97–104; Howard Thurman, "Judgment and Hope in the Christian Message," *The Christian Way in Race Relations* [New York: Harper and Brothers, 1948], 230). The story of Babel

is about the concentration of power through the facility of language. Bruegge-mann (*Genesis*, 97) suggests that "The narrative poses important issues about the practice and function of language. It suggests that all human language has become a language of disobedience." Donald Gowan argues, "The more power they are able to concentrate the more harm they will be able to do to them-selves and the world. So we ought to understand God's decision (11.7–8) as not so much the punishment of sin as a preventive act to overt great potential evil" (Donald Gowan, *Genesis 1–11: From Eden to Babel* [Grand Rapids: Eerdmans; Edinburgh: Handsel Press, 1988], 119).

19. Samuel D. Proctor, "The Pastor and Diversity, Liberation and Commu-nity," *The African American Pulpit* 1, no. 1 (Winter 1997–98): 20.

20. Robert M. Franklin, "Lost Shepherds," *Emerge* (December/January 1998): 66–69. See also Michael Eric Dyson, "Wayward Soul of the Black Church," *Chicago Tribune*, 10 March 1998, Sec. 1, p. 10; Riggins R. Earl Jr., "Keep Grace: Preaching and Church Politics," *Christian Century* 114, no. 31 (5 November 1997): 996–97.

21. Harold Cruse, *The Crisis of the Negro Intellectual: A Historical Analysis of the Failure of Black Leadership* (New York: William Morrow and Company, 1984), 13.

22. Kevin K. Gaines, *Uplifting the Race: Black Leadership, Politics and Culture in the Twentieth Century* (Chapel Hill: University of North Carolina Press, 1996), 5. Gaines refers to Darlene Clark Hine, "Rape and the Inner Lives of Black Women in the Middle West: Preliminary Thoughts on the Culture of Dissem-blance," in *Unequal Sisters: A Multicultural Reader in U.S. Women's History*, ed. Ellen Du Bois and Vicki L. Ruiz (New York: Routledge, 1990), 292–97.

23. Joy James, *Transcending the Talented Tenth: Black Leaders and American In-tellectuals* (New York: Routledge, 1997). See also Robert C. Smith, *We Have No Leaders: African Americans in the Post-Civil Rights Era* (Albany: State University of New York Press, 1996).

24. William Julius Wilson, *When Work Disappears: The World of the New Ur-ban Poor* (New York: Knopf, 1996); Cornel West, *Race Matters* (Boston: Beacon Press, 1993), 8–20.

25. Walter E. Fluker, "The Politics of Conversion and the Civilization of Friday," *Journal of the Interdenominational Theological Center* 21, nos. 1–2 (fall 1993–spring 1994): 64–80.

26. C. Eric Lincoln and Lawrence Mamiya, *The Black Church in the African American Experience* (Durham, N.C.: Duke University Press, 1990). The ques-tion of the nature and role of religion in African-American culture is a much-debated subject. Opinions regarding the origins and survivals in African-American religion have revolved around the theses of Melville Herskovits and E. Franklin Frazier. Herskovits argued that the slave system did not completely destroy the enslaved African's culture and that a considerable remnant of these survivals can be found in African-American religious expression (Melville Her-skovits, *Myth of the Negro Past* [Boston: Beacon Hill, 1941]). On the other hand, E. Franklin Frazier argued that "Negroes were plunged into an alien civilization

in which whatever remained of their religious myths had no meaning whatever" (E. Franklin Frazier, *The Negro Church in America;* C. Eric Lincoln, *The Black Church Since Frazier* [New York: Schocken Books, 1974], 14). Others, taking their cue from Frazier and Herskovits, have posited a form of syncretism between African-American and European-American religious experiences (Albert Raboteau, *Slave Religion* [New York: Oxford University Press, 1978], 59; Mechal Sobel, *The World They Made Together: Black and White Values in Eighteenth-Century Virginia* [Princeton: Princeton University Press, 1987]). Syncretism and reinterpretation of European-American Christianity seem to form a more tenable thesis than the extreme positions of Herskovits and Frazier. The definition of "the Black Christian tradition" offered by Peter Paris in his enlightening book, *The Social Teaching of the Black Churches* (Philadelphia: Fortress Press, 1985), best captures the distilled formulation of the many arguments for the syncretistic view and the position represented in this perspective.

27. Alasdair MacIntyre (*After Virtue*, 222) has suggested that "a living tradition . . . is an historically extended, socially embodied argument, and an argument precisely in part about the goods which constitute that tradition."

28. James M. Washington, *A Testament of Hope: The Essential Writings of Martin Luther King, Jr.* (San Francisco: Harper and Row), xi; see also Cornel West, "The Prophetic Tradition in Afro-America," in *Prophetic Fragments* (Grand Rapids: Eerdmans; Trenton: African World Press, 1988), 38–49.

29. Hans A. Baer and Merrill Singer, *African-American Religion in the Twentieth Century: Varieties of Protest and Accommodation* (Knoxville: University of Tennessee Press, 1992). The place of women in this tradition has remained largely invisible with the exception of recent research and writing such as that of Higginbotham, *Righteous Discontent;* Delores S. Williams, *Sisters in the Wilderness: The Challenge of Womanist God-Talk* (Maryknoll, N.Y.: Orbis Books, 1993); Emilie M. Townes, *Womanist Justice, Womanist Hope* (Atlanta: Scholars Press, 1993); Emilie M. Townes, ed., *A Troubling in My Soul: Womanist Perspectives on Evil and Suffering* (Maryknoll, N.Y.: Orbis Books, 1993).

30. Lawrence N. Jones, "Black Christians in Antebellum America: In Quest of the Beloved Community," *Journal of Religious Thought* 12, no. 2 (1985): 12.

31. Michael Walzer, *Thick and Thin: Moral Argument at Home and Abroad* (South Bend, Ind.: University of Notre Dame Press, 1994).

32. Howard Gardner, with the collaboration of Emma Laskin, *Leading Minds: An Anatomy of Leadership* (New York: Basic Books, 1995), 8.

33. Alasdair MacIntyre, *After Virtue*, 216; see also Stanley Hauerwas, *A Community of Character: Toward a Constructive Christian Social Ethic* (South Bend, Ind.: University of Notre Dame Press, 1981).

34. James MacGregor Burns, *Leadership* (New York: Harper and Row, 1979), 36. Burns (43–44) states, "The essence of leadership in any polity is the recognition of real need, the uncovering and exploiting of contradictions among values and between values and practice, the realigning of values, the reorganization of institutions where necessary, and the governance of change. *Essentially the leader's task is consciousness-raising on a wide plane.* . . . A congruence be-

tween the need and value hierarchies would produce a powerful potential for the exercise of purposeful leadership." In this sense, ethical leadership is transformational as opposed to transactional. Thomas E. McCollough offers one of the best succinct definitions of ethics, which makes the critical distinction between ethics and morality presented here: "Ethics is the critical analysis of morality. It is reflection on morality with the purpose of analysis, criticism, interpretation, and justification of rules, roles, and relations of a society. Ethics is concerned with the meaning of moral terms, the conditions in which moral decision making takes place, and the justification of the principles brought to bear in resolving conflicts of value and moral rules" (*The Moral Imagination and Public Life* [Chatham, N.J.: Chatham House Publishers, 1991], 5–6).

35. Here I am in agreement with virtue theorists like Alasdair MacIntyre and Peter Paris in respect to the role of institutions, traditions, practices, and habits in the development of character. Paris argues specifically that "African and African-American ethics is primarily concerned with the development of a certain kind of moral character, a character that reflects the basic values of their respective communities. Morality pertains to the cultural ethos and, hence, is culturally specific. According to this perspective there is no universal morality as such, even though some common moral values are widespread among diverse groups" (Peter Paris, *The Spirituality of African Peoples: The Search for a Common Moral Discourse* (Minneapolis: Fortress Press, 1994), 134; see chapter six for Paris's list of moral virtues: beneficence, forbearance, practical wisdom, improvisation, forgiveness, and justice.

36. Gary Wills, *Certain Trumpets: The Calls of Leaders* (New York: Simon and Schuster, 1994); Peter S. Temes, ed., *Teaching Leadership: Essays in Theory and Practice* (New York: Peter Lang, 1996), 1–12.

37. Ronald A. Heifetz, *Leadership Without Easy Answers* (Cambridge and London: Belknap Press of Harvard University, 1994).

38. See especially Jacob Heilbrunn, "Can Leadership Be Studied?" in Temes, *Teaching Leadership*, 1–13.

39. Thomas E. McCollough, *The Moral Imagination and the Public Life: Raising the Ethical Question* (Chatham, N.J.: Chatham House Publishers, 1991), 14. McCollough (19) suggests that "a meaningful discussion about values presupposes a common lifeworld, a shared cultural context within which persons respect one another and care about ideas and values as determinants of their life together."

2

Moral Development for African-American Leadership

PETER J. PARIS

The purpose of this essay is twofold. First, I will set forth the general theoretical principles underlying the ethics of moral development.[1] Second, I will relate that theory to the contemporary African-American situation, taking care to describe the basic societal problem that is presently threatening the integrity of the African-American community.

Morality pertains to the quality of life lived in human community, and ethics is its science. In other words, morality is the subject matter of ethics. Since all life lived in human community has a certain quality, and since morality pertains to that quality, all life lived in accordance with the basic values of a community of belonging is moral. According to this perspective, there is no universal morality as such. In my judgment, morality is univocal only in particular communities. For example, slaves viewed stealing from other slaves as immoral, but they did not view stealing from their slave owners as a moral issue. In short, morality is determined by the norms, values, and goals of particular communities. The resolution of conflict in relationships between and among communities requires that all concerned be in agreement with the norms, values, and goals of some transcendent community in which the conflicting groups share membership. Apart from such membership, it would not be possible to negotiate a just resolution, and thus the result would likely be continued animosity, repression of the weaker community by the stronger, varying degrees of warfare, and perhaps even genocide.

Yet, membership in a so-called transcendent community can never be a guarantee that member groups will always comply with its governing principles. This was illustrated many years ago in the repeated attempts to persuade the United Nations to expel from membership the Republic of South Africa — a nation whose constitution denied the vote to over 80 percent of its peoples, and a nation that had refused to be a signatory to the Universal Declaration of Human Rights. Ironically, perhaps, the political support of the United States and Great Britain long aided and abetted South Africa in its moral and political recalcitrance.

The long historical struggle of African Americans for full membership in the body politic constitutes our most prominent domestic example of the moral and political oppression of one group by another. Countless other examples abound, however, within the United States and around the world.

A fundamental assumption underlying my understanding of social ethics is the dialectical relationship between person and community. That is to say, personhood is established only in the context of a community of persons that in turn constitutes both a limiting condition and a liberating resource for all thought and practice. Similarly, community is constituted when persons choose to come together to create, preserve, and enhance the conditions that make possible their common life. Those conditions must include guarantees of personal security, material resources, and the freedom of public expression. I am in agreement with the theologian/philosopher Paul Tillich, who argued that the person-community dialectical relationship is ontological in nature. That is to say, it is expressive of Being itself. The reality of personhood is not possible apart from participation in community. Any radical separation of the two destroys both. Admittedly, various cultures have tended to give primacy to one or the other of these dialectical elements. For example, American culture tends to give moral primacy to the individual while African cultures tend to bestow it on the community.[2] Both tendencies generate disharmony (a life-and-death struggle) at the center of human life. Imbalance between the two can destroy the possibility of human life as such. As a consequence of these differing tendencies, however, American and African cultures have quite different understandings of such ethical matters as freedom, liberty, responsibility, law, and justice, to mention only a few.

Since there are many schools of ethics, it is important to identify the particular ethical traditions that have been most influential on my thinking as an ethicist. First and foremost, I am neo-Aristotelian in that I draw upon Aristotle's thought in several ways while taking care to augment it with many insights drawn from the enlightenment tradition of human rights, the American tradition of pragmatism, and the tradition of African spirituality, which emphasizes the unity of all life throughout the universe, that is, the life of spirit, history, and nature.

Ethics is a practical science. Its goal is knowledge of the moral good that humans can do in order to become morally good. Thus, knowing is for the sake of doing and becoming. As a practical science, ethics shares much in common with art. Unlike some arts, however, whose products can stand apart from the process of doing, ethics is like music in that its goal is not separated from the practice. There is no music apart from the playing of music, and there can be no good people apart from the practice of good actions. Good action is always purposive, and its goodness is determined by the extent to which its quality is commensurate with that of the goal it serves. Thus, clarity about the goal is the first principle of good action.

Further, ethics and politics are integrally united. The aim of ethics is to help persons become morally good, and the aim of politics is the same. Thus, like Aristotle, I think that the study of the moral life of the community is the major ethical science, while the study of how individuals become good is the minor science. The former pertains to the authoritative function of law in the formation of human community; the latter pertains to the function of socialization in small communities of belonging — family, school, church, and so forth — that are either enabled or disabled by the law. According to Aristotle, morally good persons can be morally good citizens only in a morally good state. Conversely, in a bad state, good persons cannot be good citizens.

Morality pertains to psychology.[3] The process of moral development refers to the quality of the psyche. When fully developed into a specific type of character, the psyche is known by its disposition to act in a certain way. That disposition is not given by nature but shaped by the cultivation of good moral habits. In other words, a good moral disposition pertains to the regulation of the impulses, drives, desires, passions, and appetites, and its form appears in a set of moral virtues that are acquired only by moral example and habitual practice.

The practical habits from which moral virtues emerge are not acquired easily because they involve effort and, sometimes, discomfort. Yet, as learning to play an instrument or ride a bicycle is stressful in the beginning, practice eventually renders the activity easy because it becomes a habit and can be performed without thinking. This does not imply, however, that practice is devoid of thought. Rather, thought is absorbed in habitual activity. Thus, the habit of moral practice is expressive of moral character. Once established, moral habits cannot be easily broken. Thus, neither a racist nor a misogynist can be easily changed. Thought and knowledge alone will not and cannot effect the necessary transformation. In fact, thought itself, including great ideas, changes nothing. Like all action, a change of character involves an act of the will. Will is the internal principle of motion at the center of the human being, capable of integrating the person's reasoning and appetitive functions. Accordingly, good action is reasoned practice in pursuit of a particular goal that is desired by the actor and set in motion by free choice, which I identify with the will.

Thus, the moral transformation of either a racist or a misogynist necessitates strong desire on the part of that person to do nonracist or nonmisogynist activities regularly over a long period of time. Only then can the activity become habitual and, eventually, expressive of the person's character. That is to say, others will come to view the person in question as having the disposition to act in either nonracist or nonmisogynist ways.

How are the passions shaped or reshaped to desire one type of activity while shunning another type? How do we come to love moral virtue and to hate vice? Obviously, from what has been said above, the person cannot train him/herself to become morally good in isolation from the community. That process must be undertaken in the context of community and by mentors who exemplify the community's values in their own practice. Someone has said that we do not teach what we know but *who we are*. Invariably, the latter is remembered while the former is often forgotten. Thus, when we think about the teachers whom we remember from our youth, do we not remember their character more than what they taught?

Good moral character requires appropriate practice under the guidance of appropriate mentors. The extent to which one's will is brought into obedience to the practice depends on the nature of the training and the extent to which the latter gives due consideration to the fact that all moral action must be voluntary. Moral action must be freely chosen. Involuntary activity can never be moral. All reasonable people agree that no one can be blamed or praised for activity carried out under the conditions of force. This has often raised difficult moral dilemmas for soldiers who have been trained to act in obedience to the commands of their superior officers. Can they be held morally responsible for the consequences of their actions? Recently, a firefighter was reluctant to accept an award for heroism because he felt that he was merely doing his job, and thus his action was not heroic because, in his view, it was not a free act expressive of his character but a matter of duty. Some have argued that children reared under authoritarian conditions fail to learn how to exercise freedom in a morally responsible way and thus fail to become moral agents. In other words, if one has never been free to act, one will not be able to act freely should the opportunity present itself. Many of these issues were at stake in the trial of the two Menendez brothers, who confessed that they deliberately murdered their parents in self-defense because, after years of sexual abuse and intimidation, they feared that their parents intended to kill them. Others, like the parents of Patty Hearst, have sought nullification of moral culpability by claiming that the alleged brainwashing of the accused prevented that person from acting voluntarily. In a segment of the award-winning documentary film *Eyes on the Prize*, a white woman says that she had been born and raised to view black people as inferior. Nobody ever told her anything different. Thus, it was not until she later discovered evidence to the contrary that she began the long process of self-transformation.

Moral training must give due consideration to the nature of freedom and its primacy in moral action. Even under the conditions of coercive training procedures, as in the military, serious consideration must be given to bringing the will of the recruits into compliance with the dictates of their training. Otherwise, the soldier will not willingly affirm the training and may fail to apply it well in a crucial moment of decision making. Many techniques are employed to effect this goal, with soldiers constantly being informed that their personal lives, the lives of their comrades, and the life of their nation are always at stake, and that the faithful performance of their duty is a matter of life and death for themselves and their nation. Thus, the instinct of self-preservation is harmonized with the loftier spirit of patriotism, and therein lies the final praise both for those who survive the battle and those who die in the line of duty. Both are duly praised for their courage, which in the military is the paramount moral virtue.

The process of moral training is not totally dissimilar from that of military training, even though the means may be quite different in many respects. Communal stability and consistent training in the community's values are two necessary elements for moral formation. Both begin in the primary community of nurture, which is either the biological family or a surrogate family. The level of trust and mutual respect between the child and his/her parents, guardians, and other mentors determines the efficacy of the process, that is, the extent to which the child eventually internalizes the moral training and makes it part of him/herself.

As implied previously, because persons are not moral by nature, moral formation must struggle against natural instincts in order to bring them under the control of the will. We should note, however, that although persons are not moral by their nature, neither is their nature opposed to moral formation. Rather, depending on the quality of their community, their characters can be formed in good or bad ways; they can be formed either for the purpose of maintaining and enhancing the moral goals of their community or the contrary.

Although all persons desire pleasure and resist pain, the process of moral training must include appropriate merits and demerits. In appropriate ways, the community must demonstrate its pleasure with those who become moral and show its displeasure with those who resist moral formation. If used properly, praise and blame (merit and demerit) are the most effective motivating forces in the process of moral formation. Yet, I cannot emphasize too strongly this important fact: the demerits must always be in the service of aiding the person towards moral improvement rather than alienating the person from the process of moral formation. When demerits become mere punishment, they serve the goal of alienation and, concomitantly, attitudes of disloyalty, disrespect, disaffection, and dissension are formed.

The family is the primary locus for moral formation because it has virtually exclusive control over the child's formative period of growth and development. During the early years of the child's life, the family determines how, when, and to what extent the child will be exposed to cognate institutions such as day care centers, schools, churches, and the like. A major moral travesty occurs, however, when families become dysfunctional and/or discover that they cannot find the appropriate cognate institutions needed for the ongoing development of their children. For example, if the values of the family situation are not in harmony with those of school and church, the child will likely experience moral confusion and fail to grow in a morally consistent way. Probably, various disciplinary problems in each context will evidence that confusion.

In earlier times and in societies simpler than our own, the family, school, and church shared a common moral ethos. For example, under the conditions of racial segregation in the United States, Canada, South Africa, and elsewhere, black families, schools, and churches also shared a common moral ethos. Under those conditions, parents, teachers, and clergy functioned as moral exemplars because they embodied the community's basic values and, by precept and example, transmitted them effectively from one generation to the other. Thus, in the midst of a hostile white world, a black world of moral integrity was created and maintained by the united forces of black families, black schools, and black churches. Unwittingly, the destruction of racial segregation as a principle of dehumanization has greatly threatened the principle of humanization that emerged within the veil of segregation. The desegregation of public schools has resulted in the general demise of the black moral ethos in the public schools, and so students experience the public schools as unfriendly, alien spaces not primarily interested in their well-being. Public schools are experienced as out of sync with the values of black families, churches, and the larger black community. Recognition of this problem has led a growing number of black churches to form their own schools. Yet, private education can never compete with public education in providing blacks with universal access to education, and therein lies a major political problem. This moral issue is a permanent inheritance destined to affect the moral formation of African Americans for the foreseeable future. Private black schools may provide the few with more favorable conditions than racially integrated schools for improved self-esteem and the realization of their educational goals. But the class bias implicit in such models invariably leads to elitism while the racism of public schools remains unchecked.

In addition to the demise of segregated black schools, black families have also been hard hit by the conditions of urban poverty and the seriously flawed housing and welfare systems of the federal government, all of which have served to weaken the moral ethos of all black families — a weakening that has been exacerbated by the flight of the black middle class from the inner cities. Thus, among the black urban poor especially, the basic conditions for moral formation are greatly threatened. These include communal stability and the consistent training of children in accordance with the community's basic values. Helping to reconstruct stable families and trustworthy schools in the black community is the most difficult political challenge facing all concerned citizens in this final decade of the twentieth century.

Let us not suppose that the middle-class black family represents moral health. On the contrary, transplanted to the suburbs, the black middle class has also been negatively affected by the demise of segregated schools whose primary aim was to produce men and women dedicated to using their talents and skills for the good of the black community. Historically, these were destined to be "race leaders," the community's highest praise for its heroes. Surprisingly, a growing number of so-called successful middle-class blacks seem to take great pleasure in assuming a Horatio Alger disposition for themselves, thus implying that they owe the African-American community nothing in return for their social and economic progress. Such a portrayal was seen clearly in the character of Justice Clarence Thomas as he aspired to the Supreme Court as the successor of Justice Thurgood Marshall. These two persons represent moral contraries. Thomas shuns the notion of "race leadership"; Marshall embodied it. The major dilemma facing the middle-class black family is whether or not it will expend the energy to provide the necessary conditions for the nurture of its children in the black moral ethos.

In summary, moral formation necessitates moral communities and moral exemplars within those communities. If moral formation in the African-American tradition is to be efficacious, the family, the school, the church, and other related institutions must share a common moral ethos. Otherwise, African-American men and women either will be morally formed in accordance with other traditions or will become morally confused persons.

Now moral formation is a necessary but not sufficient condition for leadership, religious or otherwise. Not all morally formed persons become leaders, yet most should, even though leadership implies the cultivation of additional characteristics. Along with being moral, leaders must understand the rules on which moral practice is based and be able to guide the actions of others in accordance with those guidelines. Moral leaders not only must have the capacity to regulate their own lives in accordance with moral virtue, but also must be able to lead others to do likewise. In other words, they must display the capacity for good judgment, that which Aristotle called "practical wisdom."[4] It is a mental capacity that is perfected by the habit of making good judgments. While moral virtue pertains to the excellent regulation of the appetites, moral judgment (practical wisdom) pertains to the excellent regulation of the intellect, which in turn provides the reasoning powers underlying the moral virtues. Thus, good moral leadership requires a mind trained in the art of making good judgments, which cannot be acquired in classrooms alone but also in various types of practices.

Now the training for African-American moral leadership necessitates the identification of potential leaders. These are readily discernible in many varying contexts, for example, on kindergarten playgrounds, on sports teams, in youth organizations, and in schools. Contrary to the views of many, especially those of youth, however, good leaders may or may not be the most popular people among their peers. Yet, their supporters must be able to see their superior abilities and have confidence that they will honor the community's trust by giving priority in all their actions to the community's well-being. Disdain always results when people discern that their leaders have betrayed their trust.

Thus, good leaders are those who faithfully embody the basic traditions and values of those who are being led, and who have the ability to inspire the loyalty of the latter. As implied previously, the development of good leaders requires a communal context wherein teachers are exemplars of the desired goal, and wherein the willing association between teachers and students engages all in the process of constructing a common life through common work, study, recreation, and worship. Traditionally, the black churches have been the loci for the development of this type of community. Unfortunately, large numbers of our contemporary youth are estranged from the churches, in large part because the churches need to undergo serious changes in their thought and prnctice to addiuss the needs of the twenty-first century with some measure of effectiveness. If they refuse to change, they will become as irrelevant as many of the churches in European countries have become for their citizens: mere museums of dead art.

Apart from revolutionary occurrences, traditions change very gradually. As a matter of fact, institutions and organizations stubbornly resist change for pragmatic reasons. As long as the traditions work, they are respected and maintained. Change leads to anxiety about its workability, and therefore is usually resisted. For this reason, leaders are carefully assessed by their constituents in order to ensure that the leaders know, respect, and are willing to uphold all the relevant traditions. Within limits, leaders may change in their breadth and depth of knowledge and demonstrated abilities. Yet, any radical change is likely to jeopardize their effectiveness. Long terms in office are likely to ensure a high measure of institutional stability and a low level of creative advance. This observation could be tested empirically by a careful analysis of leaders who have held office for thirty to forty years or longer.

In life, Martin Luther King Jr. was viewed by the vast majority of African Americans as a leader par excellence. Similarly, Fannie Lou Hamer and countless others were widely acclaimed as moral leaders. Correspondingly, they and others like them were viewed by the vast numbers of racists as immoral enemies. This evidences that leaders embody particular traditions, and very few among them have the ability to inspire peoples of diverse traditions. Yet, none inspire all peoples. Leaders embody cultural habits and practices and traditions. Certain leadership virtues among African Americans can be easily identified — virtues that may well be applicable for all leaders everywhere. These include honesty, truthfulness, forgiveness, forbearance, courage, generosity, faithfulness (loyalty to the cause), and justice. It is difficult to think of any moral virtues that pertain to one cultural group alone, even though the content of rhetoric and styles of leadership will certainly reflect the ethos of specific peoples. In many contexts, nativity (race, gender, sexual orientation) may well be a required condition for leadership even though it is never a moral virtue per se.

Finally, African-American leaders have always exhibited various styles of leadership, which in turn have reflected different types of organizations and institutions. Yet, these leaders have shared one thing in common, namely, loyalty to the cause of serving the good of the African-American community. Traditionally, these were united by a shared moral ethos that characterized the African-American home, school, and church — the principal institutions of moral formation in the African-American community. Major changes in the nature of public schools, a general demographic shift of the black middle class, and structural changes in the economy that have eliminated the nation's need for a reserve black working class combine to make it very difficult to develop the kind of African-American leadership needed today. Contemporary moral leadership should not be limited to one type of leadership, but many types in every area of social life. Yet, all African-American leaders must be united by the reaffirmation of a common moral ethos in the search for appropriate institutional forms. If our people were able to respond to a similar call centuries ago with much more limited resources at their disposal than we now have, we can respond similarly to the needs of this generation. But meaningful response requires intelligence, imagination, creative risk, and much commitment. African-American churches were traditionally the custodians of those mental resources. The potential of those churches is still available to us, yet many continue to stand in need of hearing the battle cry to redirect their energies towards new endeavors, enlightened by new knowledge. All of their energies must be devoted to the restoration of the symbiotic relations among healthy families, good schools, vibrant churches, and committed community organizations. Surely there is no greater moral value in our day than that of developing, expanding, and enhancing moral community for the well-being of African Americans and the whole citizenry.

Notes

1. See my book, *The Spirituality of African Peoples: The Quest for a Common Moral Discourse* (Minneapolis: Fortress Press, 1994), for a full treatment of an African and African-American theory of moral virtue.

2. See *Spirituality of African Peoples*, chapter 3, which demonstrates the centrality of community in all traditional African cultures and how its preservation and enhancement determines the nature of all African thought and practice, both on the continent and throughout the African diaspora.

3. In a study of Booker T. Washington, W. E. B. Du Bois, Martin Luther King Jr., and Malcolm X, Robert M. Franklin's analysis of the way leadership styles are rooted in and expressive of personality types demonstrates the correlation between moral leadership and psychology. See his *Liberating Visions: Human Fulfillment and Social Justice in African American Thought* (Minneapolis: Fortress Press, 1990).

4. For a more detailed analysis of this concept, see my essay, "Practical Wisdom and Theological Education," in *The Education of the Practical Theologian: Responses to Joseph Hough and John Cobb's "Christian Identity and Theological Education,"* ed. Don S. Browning, David Polk, and Ian S. Evison (Atlanta: Scholars Press, 1989), 55–62.

3

Living into the Bonds of Justice
A Challenge for Ethical Leadership
into the Twenty-first Century
MARCIA Y. RIGGS

Introduction

In his State of the Union Address in January of 1996, President Clinton began in this way:

> My duty tonight is to report on the state of the union, not the state of our government, but of our American community, and to set forth our responsibilities — in the words of our founders: to form a more perfect union.
>
> We must answer here three fundamental questions. First, how do we make the American dream of opportunity for all a reality for all Americans who are willing to work for it? Second, how do we preserve our old and enduring values as we move into the future? And third, how do we meet these challenges together, as one America?[1]

I begin with President Clinton's address because it and other "texts" (such as the Republican Party's *Contract with America*) inform and form significantly the context for asking questions about ethical leadership in this country at this time. This is not to say that such texts set the terms or limits for such questions. Rather, it is to acknowledge that these texts represent present interpretations of this country's perduring cultural narratives.[2]

Roger G. Betsworth suggests that there are "four dominant American cultural narratives": (1) the biblical story of covenant, (2) the Enlightenment story of progress, (3) the story of well-being, and (4) the story of America's mission in the world.[3] The power and persistence of these narratives to shape the American moral vision derives from their grounding in the stories of the founders of this nation and their ability to legitimate the social order by being "in some way commensurate with the experience and imagination of the majority of Americans."[4] However, according to Betsworth, these dominant narratives can be and have been challenged by groups of "insider-outsiders" (such as African Americans and women). These challenges reveal the self-deception concealed by the narratives and represent attempts to "reorder the cultural vision of the majority."[5]

The aim of this project to retrieve the black church tradition "as a strategic resource in the formation of ethical leaders for national and international communities" might thus be understood as examining the attempt of a group of "insider-outsiders" to redirect the moral vision of society in the United States. At the heart of this essay is the retrieval of the challenge and constructive response to this society's dominant moral vision deriving from the counter-hegemonic narrative and ethical tradition of African-American women as a distinctive component of the black church tradition.

In this essay, I will use this threefold method of ethical reflection: description, critical analysis, and normative proposal. First, I will describe the ethical tradition of African-American women and its distinctive contribution to the black church tradition. Next, from the perspective of the African-American women's distinctive contribution to the black church tradition, I will offer a critique of that tradition as a resource for the formation of ethical leadership. Finally, I will suggest a normative proposal about the type of ethical leadership needed into the twenty-first century.

The Distinctive Contribution of the Ethical Tradition of African-American Women

African-American women have been historically, and presently are, bound together as a distinct sociohistorical group by oppression perpetrated by the interaction of ideologies of true womanhood and white racial superiority. This has meant that although African-American women and men have experienced a kind of equality in common oppression deriving from life in a racist society, the women experienced racism in a qualitatively different manner because of the additional constraints of sexism upon their lives. In fact, because of the negative interaction of race, gender, and class oppression in the lives of black women, and the conscious acknowledgment of that tridimensional oppression, regardless of their social, economic, and educational status, the ethical tradition of black women is earmarked by challenges to a racist-sexist-classist norm used to denigrate black women in particular and black people in general.

The ethical tradition of black women is evident in the public responses of black women through their participation in religion, education, and social reform. This tradition is best characterized as socioreligious because it denotes ethical reflection and moral agency deriving from the interrelationship of the religious worldview and race-gender-class consciousness of black women.[6] The general features of this tradition are

> an evaluation of the relation between economics and justice in American society; the recognition of an interrelationship between oppression of Blacks in U.S. society and other people of color; an awareness of a connection between the oppression of Blacks and women in terms of misuse of power to subvert justice; an acknowledgment of distinctive aspects of oppression for black women; a sense of racial obligation and duty; belief in both the justice of God and justice for Blacks as a command of God.[7]

Also, this socioreligious ethical tradition is prophetic in at least three senses. First, like biblical prophets, the women relate faith and history and create "a destabilizing presence, so that the system is not equated with reality, so that alternatives are thinkable, so that the absolute claims of the system can be criticized."[8] Second, it is consistent with the relationship between religion and radicalism found in the "prophetic wing" of the black church, which espouses (1) a reappropriation of the revolutionary language of the Declaration of Independence and the Constitution, (2) providential agency, (3) a theology of national redemption emphasizing social transformation through moral reform, and (4) a critique of the practices of American democracy, yet affirming a "mutual dependency between church and state" in terms of the former being the agent of Christian love and the latter the agent of social justice.[9] Third, women writing within this tradition use a prophetic hermeneutic that is inextricably bound up with the legacy of these women's conversion into Christianity as well as their appropriation of prophetic biblical traditions to judge their reality:

> Defying the laws and customs that imposed silence upon them, African-American women testified to their personal experiences and perceptions and to those they shared with their communities. Those who converted to Christianity ... took seriously the biblical injunction to "write the vision, and make it plain" (Hab. 2:2). They used the Word as both a tool and a weapon to correct, to

create, and to confirm their visions of life as it was and as it could become.[10]

A representative example of this ethical tradition is found in the following excerpts from a speech given by Anna Julia Cooper.

Where there is no vision, the people perish. Proverbs 29:18.

A nation's greatness is not dependent upon the things it makes and uses. Things without thoughts are mere vulgarities. America can boast her expanse of territory, her gilded domes, her paving stones of silver dollars; but the question of deepest moment in this nation today is its span of the circle of brotherhood, the moral stature of its men and its women, the elevation at which it receives its "vision" into the firmament of eternal truth.

It is no fault of the Negro that he stands in the United States of America today as the passive and silent rebuke to the Nation's Christianity, the great gulf between its professions and its practices, furnishing the chief ethical element in its politics, constantly pointing with dumb but inexorable fingers to those ideals of our civilization which embody the Nation's highest, truest, and best thought, its noblest and grandest purposes and aspirations.

Professing a religion of sublime altruism, a political faith in the inalienable rights of man as man, these jugglers with reason and conscience were at the same moment stealing heathen from their far-away homes, forcing them with lash and gun to unrequited toil, making it a penal offense to teach them to read the Word of God, nay, more were even begetting and breeding mongrels of their own flesh among these helpless creatures and pocketing the guilty increase, the price of their own blood in unholy dollars and cents. Accursed hunger for gold!

...But God did not ordain this nation to reenact the tragedy of Midas and transmute its very heart's core into yellow gold. America has a conscience as well as a pocket-book, and it comes like a pledge of perpetuity to the nation that she had never yet lost the seed of the prophets, men of inner light and unfaltering courage, who would cry aloud and spare not, against the sin of the nation. The best brain and heart of this country have always rung true and it is our hope today that the petrifying spirit of commercialism which grows so impatient at the Negro question or any other question calculated to weaken the money-getting nerve by pulling at the heart and the conscience may still find a worthy protagonist in the reawakened ethical sense of the nation which can take no step backward and which must eventually settle, and settle right this and every question involving the nation's honor and integrity.

It is no popular task today to voice the black man's woe. It is far easier and safer to say that the wrong is all in him. The American conscience would like a rest from the black man's ghost. It was always an unpalatable subject but preeminently now in the era of good feeling, and self-complacency, of commercial omnipotence and military glorification. It seems an impertinence as did the boldness of Nathan when he caught the conscience of the great king at the pinnacle of victorious prosperity with inglorious seizure of the ewe lamb from a man of no importance. Has not the nation done and suffered enough for the Negro? Is he worth the blood and treasure that have been spilled on his account, the heartache and bitterness that have racked the country in easing him off its shoulder and out of its conscience? ...

But God is not dead, neither doth the ruler of the universe slumber and sleep. As a nation sows so shall it reap. Men do not gather grapes from thorns or figs from thistles. To sow the wind is to reap the whirlwind.

...Does any one question that Jesus' vision would have pierced to the heart and marrow of our national problem, and what would be His teaching in America today as to *who is my neighbor?* ...

...Homogeneous or not, the national web is incomplete without the African thread that glints and ripples through it from the beginning....

...I am no pessimist regarding the future of my people in America. God reigns and the good will prevail. It must prevail. While these are times that try men's souls, while a weak and despised people are called upon to vindicate their right to exist in the face of a race of hard, jealous, intolerant, all-subduing instincts, while the iron of their wrath and bitter prejudice cuts into the very bones and marrow of my people, I have faith to believe that God has not made us for naught and He has not ordained to wipe us out from the face of the earth. I believe, moreover, that America is the land of destiny for the descendants of the enslaved race, that here in the house of their bondage are the seeds of promise for their ultimate enfranchisement and development. This I maintain in full knowledge of what at any time may be wrought by a sudden paroxysm of rage caused by the meaningless war whoop of some obscure politicians such as the real word of 'Negro domination' which at times deafens and befuddles all ears.

Negro domination! Think of it! The great American eagle, soaring majestically sunward, eyes ablaze with conscious power, suddenly screaming and shivering in fear of a little mouse colored starling, which he may crush with the smallest finger of his great claw. Yet this mad shriek is allowed to unbridle the worst passions of wicked men, to stifle and seal up the holiest instincts of good men. In dread of domination by a race whom they outnumber five to one, with every advantage in civilization, wealth, culture, with absolute control of every civil and military nerve center, Anglo-Saxon America is in danger of forgetting how to deal justly, to love mercy, to walk humbly with its God.[11]

Significantly, this socioreligious ethical tradition was institutionalized in the black women's club movement, which was formed by the late nineteenth century. This movement, the National Association of Colored Women, was formally organized in 1896, and through it African-American women became a socioreligious movement against race, gender, and class oppression. The movement (a federation of diverse women's organizations, such as prayer circles, literary societies, and professional groups) was autonomous but not unrelated to the black church tradition. As Fannie Barrier Williams, a clubwoman and journalist during the period of its early formation, wrote in 1900,

The training which first enabled colored women to organize and successfully carry on club work was originally obtained in church work.... The churches have been sustained, enlarged and beautified principally through the organized efforts of their women members. The meaning of unity of effort for the common good, the development of social sympathies grew into women's consciousness through the privileges of church work.[12]

Also, as one contemporary interpreter of the movement suggests, the black women's club movement was the black women's extension of the black church tradition; it

was the specialized political arm of black church women: the women organized homes for youth, homes for unwed mothers, purchased club houses, and provided housing for women college students, established organizations of cultural refinement for household domestics, organized political clubs, campaigned for woman suffrage and participated in a wide variety of activities designed to promote social change and advance the interests of "the Race."[13]

It is with the institutionalization of the ethical tradition of African-American women that we discern its distinctive contribution to black church tradition. At the heart of this movement's socioreligious praxis and moral vision were these three ethical terms: renunciation, inclusivity, and responsibility.[14] Renunciation derives from the ability of the black female elite leadership to recognize their commonality, create shared understanding, and work with diverse classes of women. The leaders of the movement knew that to be in solidarity with all classes of women, they had to be willing to renounce the "privilege of difference" that their class status afforded them. The renunciation of privilege can be described as a virtue that requires us to acknowledge the way we confuse achieved worth or status or socially constructed worth (based upon features of human existence such as race, ethnicity, and gender, which are often the source of conflict) with our created worthiness given by God the Creator and sustained by Jesus Christ the Redeemer. Out of the virtue of the renunciation of privilege, we discern that achieved or socially constructed difference is a direct hindrance to Christian morality when we base the whole of our worth as human beings upon it and use our differences to promote ourselves and/or structures that exclude others.

Inclusivity describes a primary value and corresponding obligation of the black women's club movement. We learn from the women that as a value, inclusivity requires the opening up of boundaries so as to realize interrelationship as a moral good. As an obligation, inclusivity mandates that we respect difference as the necessary point of departure for understanding and actualizing authentic unity. Inclusivity means that any quest for unity must be premised upon interrelationships between the different "we's" we are rather than upon homogenization to create an "us" or domination to maintain unity.

Responsibility refers to the moral agency of the club women. The club women's efforts mediated between the fulfillment of an obligation to racial uplift and a belief in the justice of God and justice for black people as a command of God. Mediating this empirical duty (racial uplift) and the faith claim (the justice of God) resulted in the movement's moral vision being one of socioreligious responsibility.[15] This moral vision of socioreligious responsibility stresses that responsible action issues from mediating ethical process whereby neither our need to address empirical realities nor our faith claims about who ultimately oversees those realities subsumes the other. These three ethical terms — renunciation, inclusivity, responsibility — as the basis for the socioreligious praxis and vision of the women's club movement are thus its distinctive contribution to the black church tradition, as the following critique of that tradition will demonstrate.

Critique of the Black Church Tradition

Peter Paris grasps the fundamental aspect of the black church's collective moral tradition when he describes "the black Christian tradition" as a principle of nonracism rooted in the biblical vision of the parenthood of God and the kinship of all peoples.[16] The black Christian tradition has been and continues to be normative for the ethical reflection and moral agency of African-American Christians. According to Paris,

> Nothing more important can be said of the black churches than that they represent the historical embodiment of a universally significant principle. That alone — an anthropological principle grounded in the biblical understanding of the nature of humanity and its relation to God — constitutes their uniqueness in American religious history. All of the functions of the black churches are attempts to mediate this theologically grounded anthropological principle with the demands of the racial situation in every period of history. This has always constituted the mission of the black churches to the larger American society.[17]

It is evident that this tradition has been operative for the black churches as participants in the abolition movement through the contemporary civil rights movement; thus it has been undergirding moral agency that facilitated racial social justice as a movement from segregation to integration. As Paris suggests, the black Christian tradition has provided the means to grapple with the demands of the racial situation in every period. The question is whether or not the tradition as articulated to date is adequate to address the present racial situation. Whereas integration sought the inclusion of black people in terms of reform within society in the United States, the struggle in this historical period is for liberation, for inclusion in terms of structural transformation of the society.

It is my contention that the black church tradition (which emphasizes the elements Paris outlines) provides necessary but insufficient moral grounding for the demands of this present racial situation, which requires liberative moral vision and agency. What is the nature of the tradition's insufficiency?

First, the black church tradition lacks an adequate consideration of the need for intragroup accountability as prerequisite to intergroup accountability, which then will become the basis for liberation understood as intercommunal reconciliation. With the aid of the ethical tradition of African American women, we are reminded that the black church may have to address some internal matters in order to be an authentic force for liberative justice.

Importantly, the centrality of a belief in a just God in the ethical tradition of black women adds an explicit self-critical dimension to black church tradition. In the context of theocentric justice, both the moral character and the moral agency of the community seeking sociohistoric justice are subject to ongoing critique. One crucial aspect of this ongoing critique in the black churches that its tradition has failed to address is gender relations. As womanist Christian social ethicist Emilie Townes frames the matter,

> The task of the black church in building a house to come home to must take gender analysis seriously. The essential space the black church can provide is one which welcomes *and* challenges.... [A womanist ethic of justice] challenges African-American men to address sexist rhetoric and actions.
>
> Within the church and without, African-American women and men are competing for life. This competition is a cruel wage on scarce resources in a hegemonic culture and social structure. Playing this wager means settling for an imposed hierarchy in which only one gender's concern is addressed at a time. The result is a praxiological disaster and an endangered community. A community affirms the worth of the people who are in it and invites others to join it because it offers life and health. To set up a hierarchy of needs based on femaleness and maleness is shortsighted and discriminatory. This lives out the model of the white power structure and the white version of Christianity that condones oppression.[18]

In other words, if the black church is to nurture ethical leaders who demand and do racial justice in society, then that church must embody gender justice. When women and men in the black church mediate our faith claim about there being neither male nor female in Christ and the empirical realities (the injustice) of being female *and* male in *the church*, we will model the justice we seek in the larger society.

A second reason for retrieving the ethical tradition of African-American women is to correct the distorted moral vision of the black church tradition. Most of us would agree that the black church tradition's moral vision was articulated well by Martin Luther King Jr. as the moral vision of the beloved community. Although I think that King held in tension the struggle to be a self-determining community and the quest to actualize an inclusive, universal human community, we have collapsed that tension. In collapsing the tension, we have compromised self-determination and diversity as earmarks of a morally viable black community, and the compromise has actually become the ground for further entrenchment of injustice.

The three ethical terms — renunciation, inclusivity, and responsibility — at the heart of the moral vision of the African-American women's ethical tradition can help us to reclaim the moral vision of the beloved community. From the moral vision of African-American women, we are reminded that universalism is mediated by particularity, and that such mediation requires that we *do not* compromise the diversity of our humanity, our cultures. Instead, we must live into the tensions that our encounters with one another's diversity will create, believing that the needed moral responses will be generated through such encounters. A particular type of ethical leadership is needed to guide us through such encounters, and this is the subject of the discussion that follows.

Ethical Leadership into the Twenty-first Century: The Challenge

At the beginning of this essay, I noted that certain texts — President Clinton's 1996 State of the Union Address and the Republican Party's *Contract with America* — inform and form significantly the context for asking questions about ethical leadership in this country at this time. This is the case because these texts articulate two major ethical positions that are undergirding social policy debates and debates about justice in this country.

President Clinton's Democratic position tends to promote an ethical perspective desiring a common good. In his own words, the state of the union is about "our American community" and the quest "to form a more perfect union." The Republican position represents the individual rights ethical position. This is evident in the *Contract with America*, where these four principles are presented: (1) individual liberty, (2) economic opportunity, (3) limited government, and (4) personal responsibility.[19]

With these two ethical positions — one stressing a common good, the other individual rights — as the basis for social policy debates, the debates are often deadlocked and seem to be interminable. This is the case because the sides to the debates are characterized as liberal and conservative, respectively, and are then believed to be diametrically opposed to each other. As opponents engaging from diametrically opposed positions, the proponents of each position have heated arguments but are not engaged in authentic moral debate. In other words, as the differences between the positions are accentuated and no attempt is made to *mediate between* them, needful moral debate about trenchant policy issues cannot be initiated and sustained. As heated argument rather than genuine moral debate continues, the larger ethical task to which specific policy issues point is lost, namely, manifesting "the bonds of justice."

The "bonds of justice" is my ethical construct signifying that justice is tridimensional. Justice must always be construed as mediating the corrective, compensatory, and distributed claims of those who are oppressed. Mediation of these dimensions of justice is necessary to our life together as a society that acknowledges its wrongs, struggles to address forthrightly those wrongs, and strives for a just future constituted by ongoing redistribution of its social goods. This is a historical and processual understanding of justice that should keep us from being seduced into thinking social policy aimed at justice can desist too quickly because "it's been long enough."

From the ethical tradition of African-American women, we learn that mediating ethical process requires that both the liberal and conservative positions be heard and valued, and that neither position in and of itself is adequate. Therefore, the positions must be mediated so that a creative, more adequate ethical position can emerge.[20] This creative, more adequate ethical position regarding social policy matters may or may not include elements of the two prior positions, but it *will* mediate the corrective, compensatory, and distributive claims of justice.

Ethical leadership grounded in black church tradition corrected and extended by the ethical tradition of African-American women will embody at least the following characteristics:

1. *These leaders will be interpreters who exhibit moral courage.* They will be social-analytical interpreters of the context and knowledgeable about counter-hegemonic narratives and traditions as resources for interpretation. They will be morally courageous in that they know that moral life is an act of imagination, depending upon which images are presented as central to it.[21]

2. *These leaders will be facilitators who are guiding a process of mediating differing ethical positions so as to engender* creative *moral responses.* The leadership style will be more that of consensus builders (educating, persuading, seeking to mediate the tensions and conflicts) than that of crusaders or commanders.[22] They desire participatory democracy.[23]

3. *These leaders have committed but not absolutist moral postures, leaving themselves open to transformation in and through the very process of mediating the moral debate and agency that they are seeking to facilitate.*

Ethical leadership into the twenty-first century is about living into the bonds of justice, meeting the challenge of mediating the tensions and conflicts of empirical realities with a faith in the ongoing, ever flowing revelation of God's justice.

Notes

1. President Clinton, State of the Union Address, 24 January 1996.

2. Roger G. Betsworth, *Social Ethics: An Examination of American Moral Traditions* (Louisville: Westminster/John Knox Press, 1990), 15. Cultural narratives differ from ordinary stories told in a culture. In order to be told, a story must be set within a world. The cultural narrative establishes the world in which an ordinary story makes sense. It informs people's sense of the story in which they set the story of their own lives. The history, scriptures, and literary narratives of a culture, the stories told of and in family and clan, and the stories of popular culture all articulate and clarify the world of the cultural narrative in which they are set. Thus a cultural narrative is not directly told. Indeed, the culture itself seems to be telling the cultural narratives. As Clifford Geertz puts it, a culture *is* a historically transmitted pattern of meanings embodied in symbolic forms.

3. Betsworth, *Social Ethics*, 6–18.

4. Betsworth, *Social Ethics*, 19. The Puritans of New England were the leaders of church, state, and commerce. They told the biblical story from the perspective of the ruling class. Following the revolution, the story of the mission of America was the primary way in which the leadership interpreted the country's meaning, both to American citizens and to the world. As the center of power shifted to the emerging commercial and industrial sector, the Enlightenment story of progress was told by persons of power such as Benjamin Franklin and Andrew Carnegie. They also told the story of the mission of America in Enlightenment language. In the twentieth century, the story of well-being has been widely promulgated by those who have access to that most modern of powers, the contemporary mass media. The power to disseminate world-shaping stories has continued to be the privilege of the powerful, who have shaped the culture according to their own vision.

5. Betsworth, *Social Ethics*, 8–21.

6. Cheryl Townsend Gilkes writes, "As a worldview it encompasses mythic, experiential, doctrinal, ethical, ritual, and social dimensions, and transcends specific organizational or denominational forms" ("Religion," in *Black Women in America: An Historical Encyclopedia*, ed. Darlene Clark Hine [Brooklyn: Carlson Publishing, 1993], 967).

7. See my article, "The Socio-Religious Ethical Tradition of Black Women: Implications for the Black Church's Role in Black Liberation," *Union Seminary Quarterly Review* 43 (1989): 119–32.

8. Walter Brueggemann, "The Prophet As a Destabilizing Presence," in *A Social Reading of the Old Testament*, ed. Patrick D. Miller (Minneapolis: Fortress Press, 1994), 223.

9. Derek Q. Reeves, "Beyond the River Jordan: An Essay on the Continuity of the Black Prophetic Tradition," *Journal of Religious Thought* 2, no. 47 (winter–spring 1990–91): 42.

10. Frances Smith Foster, *Written by Herself: Literary Production by African American Women, 1746–1892* (Bloomington: Indiana University Press, 1993), 1–2.

11. Anna J. Cooper, "The Ethics of the Negro Question," Address to the Biennial Session of the Friends' General Conference at Asbury Park, N.J., 5 September 1902, Anna J. Cooper Papers, Manuscript Division, Moorland-Spingarn Research Center, Howard University, Washington, D.C. Cooper (1858–1964) was born a slave in North Carolina and later became an educator and principal in the Washington, D.C. public schools. The entire address can be found in Marcia Y. Riggs, ed., *Can I Get a Witness? Prophetic Religious Voices of African American Women: An Anthology* (Maryknoll, N.Y.: Orbis Books, 1997).

12. Fannie Barrier Williams, "The Club Movement among Colored Women of America," in *A New Negro for a New Century* (New York: Arno Press, 1969), 383.

13. Cheryl Townsend Gilkes, "The Role of Women in the Sanctified Church," *The Journal of Religious Thought* 43 (spring–summer 1986): 35.

14. For a full ethical analysis of the black women's club movement, see my book, *Awake, Arise and Act: A Womanist Call for Liberation* (Cleveland: Pilgrim Press, 1994), chapters 4–6.

15. The mediating process at the heart of this moral vision refers "more to the *process* of acknowledging seemingly diametrically opposing positions and *creating* a response that in effect interposes and communicates *between* the opposing sides. This interposition and communication between the opposing sides may be best understood as *living in tension with* rather than as aiming at an end result of integration, compromise, or reconciliation of such. Integration, compromise, or reconciliation may be an outcome, but *mediating as process* has occurred whether or not mediation as an end does" (Riggs, *Awake, Arise and Act*, 77).

16. Peter J. Paris, *The Social Teaching of the Black Churches* (Philadelphia: Fortress Press, 1985), 10.

17. Paris, *Social Teaching*, 17.

18. Emilie M. Townes, "Keeping a Clean House Will Not Keep a Man at Home: An Unctuous Womanist Rhetoric of Justice," in *New Visions for the Americas: Religious Engagement and Social Transformation* (Minneapolis: Fortress Press, 1993), 141.

19. Ed Gillespie and Bob Schellhas, eds., *Contract with America: The Bold Plan by Rep. Newt Gingrich, Rep. Dick Armey and the House Republicans to Change the Nation* (New York: Random House, 1994), 4.

20. See note 15 for the explanation of mediating ethical process.

21. See Sharon Daloz Parks, "Professional Ethics, Moral Courage, and the Limits of Personal Virtue," in *Can Virtue Be Taught?* (South Bend, Ind.: University of Notre Dame Press, 1993), 181–83.

22. For a discussion that delineates these different types of black church leadership styles, see Robert Michael Franklin, "The Safest Place on Earth: The Culture of Black Congregations," in *American Congregations: New Perspectives in the Study of Congregation*, vol. 2 (Chicago: University of Chicago Press, 1994), 257–84.

23. See Carol Mueller, "Ella Baker and the Origins of 'Participatory Democracy,'" in *Women in the Civil Rights Movement: Trailblazers and Torchbearers, 1941–1965* (Brooklyn: Carlson Publishing, 1990), 51–69.

4

Normative Biblical Motifs in African-American Women Leaders' Moral Discourse

Maria Stewart's Autobiography As a Resource for Nurturing Leadership from the Black Church Tradition

CLARICE J. MARTIN

It is of no use for us to sit with our hands folded, hanging our heads like bulrushes, lamenting our wretched condition; but let us make a mighty effort, and arise; and if no one will promote or respect us, let us promote and respect ourselves.[1]

Maria Stewart's stirring and impassioned injunction for African-American peoples to "make a mighty effort and arise" and to "promote and respect ourselves" was not unusual in nineteenth-century black women's moral discourse. Fueled by her disciplined Christian faith and her tireless activist fervor for women's rights and civil rights, her words, like the words of other black women leaders before and after her, functioned as a national "call to arms" for black Americans. Stewart sought to rouse women, men, and children alike to a new and "re-newed" commitment to secure and advance spiritual, moral, familial, and psychosocial health and empowerment within black communities.

Notions of black community development and "race uplift" in nineteenth-century America were a part of the "culture of resistance" required for the survival and elevation of black people. For persons committed to race uplift, the acquisition of education, for example, was not achieved for "individual gain," but to assist in the economic, political, and social improvement of all African Americans.[2]

Stewart never intended that black peoples' intracommunal nurture, development, and empowerment be achieved at the expense of their proactive resistance to and engagement with the experiences of racism and the sociological complexities arising from racism's continuing legacy on the larger American landscape.

Even the most obtuse observers had long recognized that the formidable conglomerates of power that structure American society had conspired to insure that black people were retained in an excluded, marginalized, and disenfranchised caste "at the bottom of the racial and ethnic heap, and farthest from the realization of the benefits normally to be derived from being American."[3] But more portentous was black people's indomitable and indefatigable determination and resolve to secure those benefits, and more, to respond to a higher calling and voice than those circumscribed by the limits of human transience and national interests. Some black Americans sought ever to be responding to and with the One who created peoples and nations, and so desired to ascertain and realize the divine intent for purposeful human existence in the created order. Maria W. Stewart was one of those persons.

Stewart's rousing "self-help" credo enjoining her black American compatriots to lift the heads that drooped like bulrushes and arise reflects the kind of propaedeutic hortatory that African-American women leaders in the black church tradition have promulgated for a long time in barely sufferable slave quarters, in the hush of heavy tree-shrouded clearings, amidst the dusty labors of fields and farms, within nuclear and extended family homes, in the formal and informal settings of religious instruction, from the pulpit (among the more liberal denominations) or other social or political settings, and in narrative, song, rhyme, or prayer. All of these places and strategies — and more — provided a setting or occasion for the vitalizing orations of what it means to love oneself, one's people, and one's God, and for what it means to flower and flourish within the drama of African-American human existence.

Refusing to acquiesce to passivity and inertia, Stewart's ardent rhetorical stance is paradigmatic of generations of activist black women within the black church tradition who have insisted that the marriage of personal piety and sociopolitical advancement of African-American people represents a healthy and durative alliance.

Trajectories in African-American Women Leaders' Moral Discourse within the Black Church Tradition

Maria W. Stewart is firmly rooted within the tradition of black church women whose writings, speeches, and activism exhibit the moral values, wisdom, and concerns arising from the black experience in America. These and other features of the black church tradition are often en-

gaged and advanced in contradistinction to the traditions of white supremacist and Eurocentric norms and hegemony that continue to render as dubious the full humanity of black people, while also seeking to legitimate and reinforce black people's marginality in American society.

Ethicist Katie G. Cannon outlines the challenge she faced in her academic study of theological ethics, noting that the literature and assumptions of Eurocentric theological ethics were complicit in a "conspiracy of silence" that reinforced the alleged inferiority of black people:

> When I turned specifically to readings in theological ethics, I discovered that the assumptions of the dominant ethical systems implied that the doing of Christian ethics in the Black community was either immoral or amoral. The cherished ethical ideas predicated upon the existence of freedom and a wide range of choices proved null and void in situations of oppression. The real-lived texture of Black life requires moral agency that may run counter to the ethical boundaries of mainline Protestantism... Racism, gender discrimination and economic exploitation, as inherited, age-long complexities, require the Black community to create and cultivate values and virtues *in their own terms* [italics mine] so that they can prevail against the odds with moral integrity.[4]

Continuing experiences of racism, gender discrimination, and sociopolitical exploitation have often been countered by an African-American moral discourse resonant with themes such as the equality of all persons made in the image of God *(imago Dei)*, the universal parenthood of God, liberation from all structures of oppression, empowerment in the psychosocial, political, and economic arenas, and affirmations of the rich and diverse cultural and intellectual contexts of African-American people's lives and faith.

African-American women's moral discourse, in particular, enjoins self-affirmation and self-determining power for black women who are triply marginalized by the intrinsically linked variables of gender, race, and class. Survival against these systems of oppression is a true sphere of moral life for which black women's collective moral counsel about how to endure these and other institutionalized evils has been life-giving and life-sustaining.[5]

African-American women have long recognized that when the "monster of inequality" rears its ugly head and threatens to thwart and destroy the very fabric of African-American life, it has at least three heads: racism, class bias, and male supremacy in church and so-

ciety. Patriarchal interests and androcentric assumptions about women and "women's place" have often required black women to demand social equality and justice as fervently from some of their black male counterparts as from their white American female and male antagonists.

Given their concerns about the phenomenology of multiple and interrelated forms of oppression, African-American women, as moral agents within black communities and churches, have transmitted as a notable and constructive dimension of their legacy of moral discourse an ethic that requires liberation from *all* forms of personal, communal, and systemic domination and oppression. Resisting, for example, androcentric prescriptions within the public and sacred spheres (society and church) that enjoin conformance to patriarchal norms of submissiveness, acquiescence, overdependency on and unquestioned subordination to *males qua males*, black grandmothers, mothers, sisters, and daughters have sought to nurture the paradigm wherein they work as equal partners and co-laborers with black grandfathers, fathers, brothers, and sons to foster the development and empowerment of black people.

Women in the black church tradition have used revered selections from the Hebrew Bible and New Testament to critique and refute the stereotypes that have been used to depict black people as "ignorant minstrels" or "vindictive militants."[6] Black women have also used the Hebrew Bible and New Testament traditions to affirm their inherent and equal worth as women — half of the human race — created by God to function in mutuality and partnership with men within the created order.[7]

One locus of the discussion of inequality within the black community and the black church tradition has been (and remains) the ordination of women in the church. Theologian Jacquelyn Grant is one of a number of twentieth-century women in the black church tradition who have addressed the issue of sexism and discriminate uses of power within the black church.[8] Like her eighteenth- and nineteenth-century foresisters Jarena Lee (1783–1849), Sojourner Truth (1797–1883), and Francis Ellen Watkins Harper (1825–1911), Grant's prophetic moral discourse enjoins the black church to be fully responsive to its higher calling to function fully as a truly liberative, redeemed, and inclusive community of God in Jesus Christ in the world.[9]

In spite of African-American women's continuing concerns about their experiences of the "triple jeopardy" of gender, race, and class bias, women in the black church tradition still spread wide their net of concern for black men, women, and children alike. As central bearers, transmitters, and interpreters of black culture and cultural traditions

(including religious norms and mores), black women of faith have allied personal authority and authenticating moral discourse with the claims of divine inspiration in support of the full empowerment of black people.

The speeches, biographies, spiritual autobiographies, and other cultural artifacts from nineteenth- and twentieth-century women leaders in the black church tradition such as Sojourner Truth, Anna J. Cooper, Jarena Lee, Ann Plato, Nannie Helen Burroughs, Mary McLeod Bethune, Fannie Lou Hamer, and Ida B. Wells Barnett still nurture, instruct, and provide a beacon of light for generations of African-American people. Moreover, these and other women have inspired national, communal, and personal efforts to create constructive, just, inclusive, and productive social structures and environments for black people — and for all Americans. They have used moral suasion, influence, authority, and power to construct an alternative moral landscape in which the highest and noblest aims of the human spirit could be realized — an influence that has had effects across the religious, sociopolitical, and national spectrum. They have, like all effective leaders, offered substantive blueprints for change, helped themselves and others to see, create, and access windows of opportunity, and functioned as masters of motivation and architects of personal, structural, and institutional transformation.

That the moral discourse of African-American women leaders in the black church tradition traversed the religious and sociopolitical spheres is not surprising, for African-American women could not ignore the seamless web of complex and interlocking issues that impinged upon the lives of black people.

In her reflections on the easy rapprochement between the religious and sociopolitical spheres, cultural scholar and singer Bernice Johnson Reagon observes that African-American culture provided more than "cultural data" for her work in the civil rights movement in the 1960s. Black culture provided a "process" for the forms and strategies for her activist engagements, a methodology for study, archiving, analysis, presentation, and practice. She notes of her involvement as program coordinator for the Albany Georgia Movement that it was her experience of mass meetings within the black church that informed her task as a program coordinator:

> In the civil rights movement, our base was Christian and we prayed to God, announcing our understanding of our commonness with all life in the universe, calling on that force to be with us. Then came another song and then announcements. Then

came the sermon or speech or testimonies and another song, with
singing all the way through to support the movements. . . . My culture had already educated me to be a program coordinator. I had
spent my life in gatherings, seeing people who were masters of
gathering us together to do this work.[10]

Personal and communal experiences within African-American culture often provided the method, forms, strategies, analyses, presentation, practice, and *content* of black church women's moral discourse.
Sojourner Truth's conversion to Christianity became the impetus for
her decision to change her name (Isabella, Belle, or Isabelle at her birth
in 1797). She changed her name to Sojourner Truth — Sojourner "because I was to travel up and down the land showing people their sins
and being a sign to them," and Truth "because I was to declare the
truth unto the people."[11] Her life and name became an authoritative
source of and witness to the moral discourse that propelled her onto
the national scene.

Ann Plato, a teacher in the (Black) Zion Methodist church school in
Hartford, Connecticut, produced one of the probably few collections of
essays by a black writer between 1840 and 1865.[12] The book, *Essays: Including Biographies and Miscellaneous Pieces, in Prose and Poetry*, contains
works that resonate with religious themes. Her poem, "Lines, Written upon Being Examined in School Studies for the Preparation of a
Teacher," contains some of the salient motifs that often punctuate black
Christian women's moral discourse and reflections: the summation of
the effects of spiritual conversion upon the life, the quest to possess and
impart to black youth of present and future generations spiritual, moral,
and social empowerment and well-being, the desire to discover and ful-
fill the divine purpose and will in one's life. The social and professional
context of her writings, a religious educational institution, places Plato
within an enduring tradition of women in the black church who were
convinced that the education and nurture of the whole person — mind,
body, and spirit — was requisite in any moral discourse and ideology of
empowerment. Her reflection reveals the graceful and wistful suppliance
of her prose.

Lines,
Written upon Being Examined in School Studies
for the Preparation of a Teacher

Teach me, O Lord! the secret errors of my way,
Teach me the paths wherein I go astray,
Learn me the way to teach the word of love,

For that's the pure intelligence above.
As well as learning, give me that truth forever —
Which a mere worldly tie can never sever,
For though our bodies die, our souls will live forever.
To cultivate in every youthful mind,
Habitual grace, and sentiments refined.
Thus while I strive to govern human heart,
May I the heavenly precepts still impart;
Oh! may each youthful bosom catch the sacred fire,
And youthful mind to virtue's throne aspire.
Now fifteen years their destined course have run,
In fast succession round the central sun;
How did the follies of that period pass,
I ask myself — are they inscribed in brass!
Oh! Recollection, speed their fresh return,
And sure 'tis mine to be ashamed and mourn.
"What shall I ask, or what refrain to say?
Where shall I point, or how conclude my lay?
So much my weakness needs — so oft thy voice,
Assures that weakness, and confirms my choice.
Oh, grant me active days of peace and truth,
Strength to my heart, and wisdom to my youth,
A sphere of usefulness — a soul to fill
That sphere with duty, and perform thy will."[13]

Retrieving Black Women Leaders' Moral Discourse: Methodological Issues in the "Search for the Pearl of Great Price"

Again, the kingdom of heaven is like a merchant in search of fine pearls; on finding one pearl of great value, he went and sold all that he had and bought it (Matt. 13:46).[14]

The writer of Matthew's gospel (80–90 c.e.) wanted to make a crucial point for his community regarding God's kingdom, already at work in their midst: like the merchant who sells all he or she has to purchase the pearl of great value, the person who discovers the kingdom preached by Jesus eagerly and joyfully forgoes all else in order to have the kingdom.[15]

African-American women's moral wisdom and discourse are like the pearl of great value or price. Pearls were a highly prized precious gem in the ancient world, and remain so today. The wise woman, man, and child would do well to search diligently for this immensely rich and valued stream of tradition. Natural pearls are formed when foreign particles enter the shell of an oyster, and the oyster's resistance to and sustained engagement with a particle ultimately yields something of inestimable value.[16] In the same way, black women's resistance to and sustained engagement with the complex and variegated dialectics of black womanhood in America have contributed to a tradition of moral wisdom, knowledge, and lore exceptional in its creativity, inexhaustible in its life-giving and life-empowering potential, and immeasurable in its historic and global significance.[17]

Any discussion of the retrieval of black women leaders' moral discourse within the black church tradition must take seriously the problems with conceptual definitions of leaders and leadership in the literature regarding women, particularly African-American women.

In this essay and in a large body of literary materials and other cultural artifacts within African-American culture and without, *it is a given* that black women have long been and continue to be decisive moral agents and leaders. Generations of black women have functioned as visionary, resourceful, independent, and innovative moral arbiters and exemplars in the public and private spheres.

Ethicist Walter E. Fluker observes in his report on the function of the National Resource Center for the Development of Ethical Leadership at Colgate Rochester Divinity School in Rochester, New York, that the aim of developing and nurturing leadership from the black church tradition includes within its purview "the critical appropriation and embodiment of moral traditions that have historically shaped the character and shared meanings of our [African-American] national life."[18] This aim seeks further to aid the development of persons toward their own critical appropriation and embodiment of particular knowledge and practices that result in the increase of justice and the actualization of human community. There is little question that black women have helped to frame and shape conceptual and ideological meanings of the discourse of moral leadership in black communities. Black women have themselves embodied leadership practices that foster the nurture and increase of justice and the actualization of human community — and they have done so passionately, persistently, perspicuously.

One of the greatest needs that analysts of leadership development within the black church tradition must address formally and theoretically concerns the definition and qualitative dimensions of the moral leadership development and practices that have contributed so decisively to the character and shared meanings of African-American life, including the function of gender within these modalities. The need becomes most acute when a review of nineteenth- and twentieth-century literature by and about African Americans reveals a tendency to identify "leaders" as black males.[19] Should not descriptive criteria, conceptual categories, and taxonomies that define "leaders" (including "moral" leaders) be nuanced to account for historic social inequalities and biases in the literature arising from gender differences? Should they not be qualified by critical analysis of particular contextual exigencies (personal, social, economic, or political factors)? Or by chronological variables? (Are the conceptual categories for assessing black women's ethical leadership in the nineteenth century philosophically and ideologically consistent with and parallel to those utilized in twentieth-century analyses?)[20]

The late historian Nathan Huggins was correct in his observation of African-American leadership: "At best it is a difficult matter to identify a group's leadership. We are seldom certain what we are looking for."[21] More critical attention to the "processes" of leadership development among African-American women in particular warrants further scrutiny and analysis. Huggins noted that much of African-American leadership, like that of Harriet Tubman and innumerable anonymous black men and women who helped to organize the Underground Railroad or disrupt the administration of the antebellum fugitive slave laws, is lost to us because we have been less interested in the *process* by which they were identified and accepted by others as leaders and more interested in the *hero*. Social scientific study of how and under what circumstances leadership arises in the "little community" — the family and the neighborhood — remains an important task for future investigation. "The Afro-American leader has almost always been thought of as one who had weight in the 'large community.'"[22]

Even if one accedes the need for a corrective to the Western cultural tendency toward the "masculinization" of leaders, the fact that black women *have* functioned as leaders in African-American history is well documented in the literature — even if not to the extent of that of black males.[23]

In *Black Leaders Then and Now*, Thomas Rose and John Greenya narrate the lives of three black leaders who helped to shape the modern era of the civil rights movement in the 1960s: Julian Bond, Marion Barry, and Charlayne Hunter-Gault.[24]

Barbara Reynolds, a nationally known African-American journalist on the editorial board of *USA Today*, edits the helpful publication *And Still We Rise: Interviews with 50 Black Role Models*. Among those interviewed are Maya Angelou, Mary Frances Berry, Shirley Chisholm,

Cardiss Colins, Marian Wright Edelman, Dorothy Height, and Bishop Leontine Kelly.[25]

Columbus Salley's anthology, *The Black 100*, contains a synopsis of the lives of influential Americans of African descent who have "injected new meaning and dignity into the veins of civilization" and America. The catalog lists eighty-one men and twenty-one women who participated in the quest for full freedom and equality from 1619 to 1992. One must question whether the list that purports to identify black influentials who have made a significant impact upon the lives of millions of black people (and Americans in general) over a period of four centuries is truly representative of black leaders when black women comprise less than 25 percent of the list. And what of the implications of such a list in the quest to document and retrieve black women's traditions of moral discourse?[26]

When the annals of Eurocentric history generally define "leaders" as male and of non-African descent, and when the annals of women's history (including feminist perspectives) focus mostly on white women leaders, what of the (in)adequacy of scholarship, research, and instruction devoted to the legacy of black women leaders in church and society? And what are the methodological implications for the ways in which historians of African-American cultural and religious history undertake their task if black women's leaders' lives and history continue to be marginalized? How are traditional categories of constructed leadership behaviors to be assessed in light of the complex texture of black women's lives and history, particularly with reference to the retrieval of African-American women's moral discourse? Surely, the "search for the pearls of great price" of black women's moral discourse traditions must proceed with all diligence and dispatch.

The Distinctive Contributions of Black Women's Ethical Leadership: Womanist Perspectives

The subject of womanist ethical, theological, and biblical interpretation has come to the fore in recent years in conjunction with the growing body of literature on "womanist theology" in general. The term *womanist* was coined by Alice Walker in her book *In Search of our Mothers' Gardens*. Describing the courageous, audacious, and "in charge" behavior of the black woman, the term *womanist* affirms black women's connection with both feminism and with the history, culture, and religion of the African-American community. Womanist literature represents the ongoing academic work of womanist scholars in a variety of disciplines, including theology, ethics, sociology, and biblical studies.[27]

It is in response to the question, "What are the social sources and functions of moral wisdom which the [black church] tradition has imparted to generations of national leaders?"[28] that womanist biblical and theological reflection may be most useful in discussions of the genesis and formulation of ethical leadership among African-American women. Three points can be made here as tentative working hypotheses.

First, womanist biblical and theological thought is itself a prime source of moral wisdom in the nurture of national ethical leaders because a number of contemporary, self-designated womanist religion scholars have sought to identify and recover black women's moral discourse traditions within the writings of pre-twentieth-century and twentieth-century black women writers. The critical reflections and insights of these womanist scholars contribute to and enlarge the ongoing stream of black women's moral discourse traditions.[29]

Second, a number of womanist religion scholars have taken seriously the supposition that for many African Americans, the Bible has functioned as one of the highest (if not *the* highest) source of authority in developing and delivering a black moral praxis and theology, and they have sought to document and interpret black women's use of the Bible.[30] The selective use of Hebrew Bible and New Testament traditions has enabled black women to refute traditions in Western culture that have been used to depict black people as ontologically inferior persons "doomed to a life of servitude" or "second class citizenship." The stories of Jesus and Jesus' affirmative encounters with women have empowered black women to deal with "the overwhelming difficulties of overworked and widowed mothers, or underworked and anxious fathers, of sexually exploited and anguished daughters, or prodigal sons, and of dead or dying brothers whose networks of relationality are rooted deeply in the Black community. Black feminist consciousness and moral values grow out of and expand upon Black, biblical experience and hermeneutics."[31]

Third, the interweaving of black women's religious, biblical, theological, and sociopolitical thought and reflection as it often emerges in autobiography, biography, and other narrative forms, documents processes of emergent transformation wherein one can chart the evolution of the Afro- or Afra-American self evolving from the more "private" citizen to the more "public" social and religious activist and ethical leader. The spiritual autobiography of Maria W. Stewart, for example, the *Productions of Mrs. Maria W. Stewart* (1835), provides a compellingly stirring lens through which the reader can observe Stewart's personal

journey and her evolution as an ethical leader whose spirited rhetoric challenged the pernicious and widespread nineteenth-century racial
suffering and evil that she encountered. A key feature of this evolution
was her skillful use of incisive hermeneutical skills and praxiologically
nuanced biblical and theological discourse to advance a moral ethic
mandating that justice become actualized, and thus, more than an idyl-
lic dream for "those of a sable hue" in America. Womanist biblical
scholars are seeking to recover and identify the hermeneutical strategies
used by black women like Maria Stewart.[32]

An important area for future exploration for persons interested
in the relationship between womanist thought and the development
of ethical leadership is the identification of historical and normative
themes in the literature of the (still emerging) disciplines of womanist
sociopolitical, literary, biblical, theological, and ethical thought. Critical
analyses of the significance of these data for the historic development
of ethical leadership among African-American peoples in general, and
within the black church tradition in particular, will be requisite for
advancing our understanding of the ideological and conceptual dimensions of ethical leadership development in the black diaspora. Such
analyses will also provide clues for how to address a wide array of
pressing familial, sociopolitical, economic, and theological issues within
black communities in our times.

Normative Biblical Motifs in Maria Stewart's Moral Discourse: Prescriptions for "Arising, Promoting, and Respecting Ourselves"

Maria Stewart's dual exhortation, "let us make a mighty effort, and
arise," and "let us promote and respect ourselves," highlights her signal
conviction of black Americans' ability to guide the ship of their own
destiny into a future of possibility, promise, and prosperity.[33] Her vision
of racial uplift, resolve, and fortitude needed for the task affirms that
in her view, African Americans should be the principal directors and
actors negotiating the dramatic action of their ever evolving journey on
the stage of life.

When one undertakes the search for the "pearl of great price" in
Maria Stewart's moral discourse, she or he encounters an embarrass-
ment of riches in Stewart's *Productions of Mrs. Maria W. Stewart*.[34] As
is characteristic of nineteenth-century black women's spiritual autobiographies, Stewart's reflective tome interweaves her thoughts about the
spiritual pilgrimage of the self with the social exigencies of her existence

as a black woman of that period in America. Profound religious faith and emphatic social activism were united in one voice in the narrative rhetoric of the medium of spiritual autobiography.[35]

It is appropriate to speak of "normative biblical motifs" in Stewart's moral discourse, for Stewart's personal piety and general worldview were nurtured in the incubator of the black religious tradition. The black church tradition played a decisive role in her spiritual and vocational formation. At the age of five, she was orphaned and "bound out" to a minister's family. She attended Sabbath schools from the ages of fifteen to twenty, and married James W. Stewart in 1826. Widowed in 1829, after a marriage of only three years, she "was brought to the knowledge of the truth, as it is in Jesus" in 1830, and in 1831, "made a public profession of [her] faith in Christ."[36]

Influenced by Reverend Thomas Paul (1773–1831) of Boston's African Baptist Church, and abolitionist apologist David Walker (1785–1830), the son of a free black mother and a slave father, Stewart gave herself to a ministry of religious and political witness:

> From the moment I experienced the change, I felt a strong desire, with the help and assistance of God, to devote the remainder of my days to piety and virtue, and now possess that spirit of independence, that, were I called upon, I would willingly sacrifice my life for the cause of God and my brethren.[37]

It is not incidental that Stewart's first-person narrative employs what is likely a biblical simile of "heads hanging down like bulrushes" to depict the state and spirit of some African Americans who, no doubt, were periodically fatigued from the continuing struggle against racial strife, discouraged by the slow and costly progress of liberty, and wearied by "the hissing and reproach among the nations of the earth against us."[38] Not only was Stewart's spiritual and theological formation embedded within the black church tradition, Stewart was an avid student of both the Hebrew Bible and the New Testament. She frequently interwove texts from the Bible, particularly the Hebrew Bible, throughout her sermons, political essays, and lectures.

It is quite plausible that Stewart drew upon allusions to bulrushes (Hebrew: *agmon*) in the Hebrew Bible for her simile. Isaiah 58:5, which describes the kind of worship that Yahweh requires of Israel, most closely resembles Stewart's use of the phrase, "bowing the head like a bulrush."

> Is such the fast that I choose,
> a day to humble oneself?

> *Is it to bow down the head like a bulrush* [italics mine],
>   and to lie in sackcloth and ashes?
> Will you call this a fast,
>   a day acceptable to the Lord?

Additional allusions to bulrushes in the Hebrew Bible are sparse (Exod. 2:3; Isa. 18:2), and in some versions the term is used interchangeably with "reed" (Hebrew: *qaneh* — as in 2 Kings 18:21; Job 8:11–14; Isa. 19:6–7, 15).

Signally, bulrushes — widespread in the Middle East — required specific conditions for growth because of their fragile stems, and thus they became symbolic of weakness, vulnerability, lowliness, and insignificance. Conversely, they could be used as a symbol of abundance and blessing (Isa. 35:7).[39]

For Stewart, the simile of the bulrush may have aptly captured the experiences of discouragement and vulnerability that may have at times assailed even the most determined black Americans during the nineteenth century. No doubt, she witnessed the vicissitudes of her struggling compatriots, the "benighted sons and daughters of Africa who have enriched the soils of America with their tears and blood."[40] But Stewart averred that the harsh realities of slavery could not prevail. Like the best of leaders in the black church tradition before her and after, she would use her influence to siren the call that would motivate and inspire all who heard her to strive for personal and communal empowerment and social change.

As noted previously, biblical narratives have often undergirded and interfused black women's moral wisdom traditions and aided in the development and nurture of a black moral theology and praxis. A number of salient and normative biblical motifs recurring in black women's moral discourse warrant closer scrutiny.

By "normative biblical motifs" is meant those motifs or themes (central or dominant ideas) in the Hebrew Bible and the New Testament that tend to recur in the biblical writings, and which appear to clarify and illumine the distinctive message and theology of a writing, while also transcending in significance the particular contingencies of that writing. In the Hebrew Bible, such normative motifs might include: the people of God (covenant community), the fear of God, Yahweh's faithfulness to Israel, Yahweh's steadfast love *(hesed)*, and the obligations for God's people to live in right relationship with neighbor and community by fulfilling the ethical call and mandate to exhibit justice and righteousness.

In the New Testament, normative biblical motifs are as wide-ranging

as those in the Hebrew Bible, and may include the summons to repentance, notions of the reign of God, Christian missionary preaching
(*euangelizo*), ethical injunctions and parenesis (ethical admonitions —
these may be eclectic in nature without reference to concrete situa-
tions) enjoining assistance to the poor, the sick or the marginalized,
and an ethic of love and care for the neighbor.

There are two normative biblical motifs recurring in Maria Stewart's
moral discourse in her spiritual autobiography (inclusive of her writings
and speeches) that serve as helpful prescriptions to black Americans to
heed her charge to "arise, promote, and respect ourselves." They are
(1) the need for personal, familial, and communal moral regeneration,
and (2) the recognition that Christian faith and an ethic of socioeconomic care, nurture, and empowerment are requisite for members
of the human family.

First, the Hebrew Bible and the New Testament enjoin the need for
moral regeneration, with an emphasis on faith and obedience to God.
In the Torah, "covenant," a primary symbol for the divine-human relationship initiated by Yahweh with Israel, includes a focus on Israel's
response to and relationship with Yahweh. Israel is to live as a "holy
nation" (Exod. 19:6), and to love God with all of the heart, soul, and
might (Deut. 6:5). The Creator alone is to be worshipped as Sovereign
(Ps. 22:27–29), and knowledge of God's saving deeds is to be passed
on from generation to generation (Exod. 12:24–27; Ps. 78:1–8). Moral
obedience to God included a commitment to honor God with the heart,
and not only the mouth (Isa. 29:13). The whole person is to respond
to God's love, for "to know Yahweh means to respond to the claim
Yahweh makes upon one's devotion."[41]

In the New Testament, the response to the good news that the kingdom (*basilea*) or dominion of God has come near in Jesus is repentance
(*metanoia*). John the Baptist heralds this cry in his messianic preaching
of Jesus: "Repent, for the kingdom of heaven has come near" (Matt.
3:2; cf. Mark 1:4; Luke 3:3). Repentance involves a new attitude, de-
manded in response to God's offer of salvation — a new orientation of
the life. More than a return to God only, it is a "call to decision" that
includes devotion to God and is consequential for the way one con-
ducts life (Luke 3:8; 10–12). It includes moral regeneration that issues
in a new attitude, new heart, new works, and a transformation of the
individual.[42]

The Pauline ethical traditions and parenesis similarly emphasize an
all-encompassing, fundamental transformation of the person who re-
sponds to God's claim upon her or his life. The liberation and new
being that come through Christ mean that Christians are now to do all

things to the glory of God (1 Cor. 10:31). Pauline parenesis admonishes the Christian to live in accordance with what the faith declares her or him to be in Christ (Rom. 6:1–14; 8:12–13; 1 Cor. 5:7–8). It addresses the whole person — the new being in Christ *as a whole* is at stake.[43]

Maria Stewart's moral discourse includes a focus on the need for moral regeneration and empirical conduct that reflect a new orientation in life. In one place, she outlines her concerns about the need for black American women, men, and children to cultivate the "pure principles of piety, morality, and virtue."

> O that my head were waters, and mine eyes a fountain of tears, that I might weep day and night, for the transgressions of the daughters of my people. Truly my heart's desire and prayer is, that Ethiopia might stretch forth her hands unto God. But we have a great work to do. Never, no, never will the chains of slavery and ignorance burst, till we become united as one, and cultivate among ourselves the pure principles of piety, morality and virtue.... O, ye daughters of Africa, awake! awake! arise! no longer sleep nor slumber, but distinguish yourselves. Show forth to the world that ye are endowed with noble and exalted faculties. O, ye daughters of Africa! what have ye done to immortalize your names beyond the grave? what examples have ye set before the arising generation? what foundation have ye laid for generations yet unborn?... And our sons, do they bid fair to become crowns of glory to our hoary heads? Where is the parent who is conscious of having faithfully discharged his duty, and at the last awful day of account, shall be able to say, here, Lord, is thy poor, unworthy servant, and the children thou hast given me? And where are the children that will arise, and call them blessed?[44]

Stewart's passion for the training of black youth in the traditions of Christian piety recurs with some regularity. Her concern for the spiritual and moral health of future generations of African-American families was unshakable. As was noted previously of Ann Plato, Stewart wished for African-American youth a belief in the "reality in religion" and "a beauty in the fear of the Lord."

> Raise up sons and daughters unto Abraham, and grant that there might come a mighty shaking of dry bones among us, and a great ingathering of souls. Quicken thy professing children. Grant that the young may be constrained to believe that there is a reality in religion, and a beauty in the fear of the Lord. Have mercy on the benighted sons and daughters of Africa.... It is you that

must create in the minds of your little girls and boys a thirst for knowledge, the love of virtue, the abhorrence of vice, and the cultivation of a pure heart. The seeds thus sown will grow with their growing years; and the love of virtue thus early formed in the soul will protect their inexperienced feet from many dangers. O, do not say, you cannot make anything of your children; but say, with the help and assistance of God, we will try. Do not indulge them in their little stubborn ways; for a child left to himself, bringeth his mother to shame.[45]

A second normative biblical motif advocates care for others, whether within the faith community or without. Often integral in this ethic is the use of material, economic, and other resources to meet concrete and existing needs, and thus to enhance the quality of life of others.

The Pentateuch (the first five books of the Hebrew Bible), for example, contains traditions that present the ideals of the community. Many of the legal codes in particular enjoin members of the covenant community to reflect a way of life that mirrors the compassionate and merciful character of Yahweh. Protecting and enhancing the well-being of those who are socially or economically marginalized or isolated within the social order, including widows, orphans, resident aliens, and debtors (Exod. 22:21, 22–24; Lev. 19:9–10, 33–34) is one of a number of moral priorities. Torah legislation forbids the people from taking advantage of the situation in which the poor find themselves, and it prescribes structural and practical ways in which the wealthy can assist the poor — the prevention of the unjust treatment of persons is in view.[46] This concern for the well-being of persons recurs throughout the Hebrew Bible.

New Testament traditions enjoining a concrete ethic of care and empowerment for those in need within the social order are equally extensive. In the preindustrial, largely agrarian Mediterranean milieu of the first century, there were many opportunities to assist in the alleviation of deprivation, suffering, and other physical and social needs.

Luke's programmatic announcement of the inauguration of Jesus' ministry declares that Jesus is bringing "good news to the poor," the proclamation of "release to the captives," "recovery of sight to the blind," and "freedom for the oppressed" (Luke 4:18–19). According to Luke, the infant church is distinguished by its care for the needs of its members (Acts 2:43–47; 4:32–37). For Luke, "the elimination of injustice and the alleviation of the sufferings of the poor and destitute, is not merely an eschatological reality, but it is a vital constituent of Christianity in this world, here and now."[47]

The Pauline corpus indicates that Paul is anchored in the practical awareness of the need for a concrete ethic in addressing socioeconomic needs within the first-century Christian communities. Paul took up a collection for the poor of the Jerusalem church (1 Cor. 16:1; 2 Cor. 8:1–7; 9:1–2; Rom. 15:25–26), an indication that he took seriously his avowed commitment to remember the poor (Gal. 2:10).

Maria Stewart's ethic of care is informed by her ardent Christian faith, for she takes seriously the integrity of human beings as made purposefully by God in the image of God. She observes of black Americans,

> Many think, because your skins are tinged with a sable hue, that you are an inferior race of beings; but God does not consider you as such. He hath formed and fashioned you in his own glorious image, and hath bestowed upon you reason and strong powers of intellect. He hath made you to have dominion over the beasts of the field, the fowls of the air, and the fish of the sea. He hath crowned you with glory and honor; hath made you but a little lower than the angels... he hath made all men free and equal. Then why should one worm say to another, "Keep you down there, while I sit up yonder; for I am better than thou?" It is not the color of the skin that makes the man, but it is the principles formed within the soul.[48]

For Stewart, there was no contradiction between a fervent passion for spiritual *metanoia* and a fervent passion for the material and economic self-development of black people in nineteenth-century America. *Both* were required for the religious and psychosocial well-being of black families and communities. As historian Gayraud Wilmore observes, the practical use of religion in all of life, the surrender of excessive individualism for solidarity with the community and nature, and the corporateness of society and all life are among the most valuable and enduring contributions of the religious traditions of Africans and African Americans.[49]

Stewart's concern for justice, wholeness, and healing in the human family is explicit in her admonition for black Americans to promote their socioeconomic well-being. Citing the example of women in Wethersfield, Connecticut, whose entrepreneurial vision prompted them to work together to raise enough money to build a church, she invites black women around her to engage in similar entrepreneurial endeavors.

> The good women of Wethersfield, Conn. toiled in the blazing sun, year after year, weeding onions, then sold the seed and procured

money enough to erect them a house of worship; and shall we not imitate their examples, as far as they are worthy of imitation? Why cannot we do something to distinguish ourselves, and contribute some of our hard earnings that would reflect honor upon our memories, and cause our children to arise and call us blessed? Shall it any longer be said of the daughters of Africa, they have no ambition, they have no force? By no means. Let every female heart become united, and let us raise a fund ourselves; and at the end of one year and a half, we might be able to lay the corner-stone for the building of a High School, that the higher branches of knowledge might be enjoyed by us; and God would raise us up, and enough to aid us in our laudable designs.[50]

In one of her most eloquent and fiery pleas for black self-help and entrepreneurial commitment, Stewart laments the fact that black women's labor largely benefits white Americans. Identifying several practical strategies for developing black economic initiative and productivity, she charges all who hear her to adopt an indomitable spirit marked by unity, knowledge, love, fortitude, and independence.

How long shall the fair daughters of Africa be compelled to bury their minds and talents beneath a load of iron pots and kettles? Until union, knowledge and love begin to flow among us. How long shall a mean set of men flatter us with their smiles, and enrich themselves with our hard earnings; their wives' fingers sparkling with rings, and they themselves laughing at our folly? Until we begin to promote and patronize each other. Shall we be a by-word among the nations any longer? Shall they laugh us to scorn forever? Do you ask, what can we do? Unite and build a store of your own, if you cannot procure a license. Fill one side with dry goods, and the other with groceries. Do you ask, where is the money? We have spent more than enough for nonsense, to do what building we should want. We have never had an opportunity of displaying our talents; therefore the world thinks we know nothing. And we have been possessed of by far too mean and cowardly a disposition, though I highly disapprove of an insolent or impertinent one. Do you ask the disposition I would have you possess? Possess the spirit of independence. The Americans do, and why should not you? Possess the spirit of men, bold and enterprising, fearless and undaunted. Sue for your rights and privileges. Know the reason that you cannot attain them. Weary them with your importunities. You can but die, if you make the attempt; and we shall certainly die if you do not.[51]

Stewart's moral discourse serves as an invaluable resource for nurturing leadership from the black church tradition and for illumining the possibilities of the noblest and most humane strivings of the human spirit under God. For Stewart, folded hands, hanging heads, and lamentation must give way, by "mighty effort," to arising, promoting, and respecting African-American life and promise. Surely her words comprise a welcome refrain, vision, challenge, and guide for African Americans now on the threshold of a march into the twenty-first century.

Notes

1. Maria W. Stewart, in her speech "Religion and the Pure Principles of Morality: The Sure Foundation on Which We Must Build." The speech was delivered in Boston in 1831, and is found on page 15 of her autobiography, *Productions of Mrs. Maria W. Stewart*, presented to the First African Baptist Church and Society of the City of Boston (Boston: Friends of Freedom and Virtue, 1835); reproduced in *Spiritual Narratives*, Schomburg Library of Nineteenth-Century Black Women Writers, ed. Henry Louis Gates Jr. (New York: Oxford University Press, 1988), 3–98. All quotations of Stewart's autobiography will be taken from the Schomburg edition.

2. Patricia Hill Collins, *Black Feminist Thought: Knowledge, Consciousness, and the Politics of Empowerment* (New York: Routledge, 1990), 147–48. On the role of the ideology of "uplift" in nineteenth- and twentieth-century women's activist endeavors, see Linda M. Perkins, "Heed Life's Demands: The Educational Philosophy of Fanny Jackson Coppin," *Journal of Negro Education* 51, no. 3 (1982): 181–90; and "The Impact of the 'Cult of True Womanhood' on the Education of Black Women," *Journal of Social Issues* 39, no. 3 (1983): 17–28.

3. C. Eric Lincoln, *Race, Religion, and the Continuing American Dilemma* (New York: Hill and Wang, 1984), 14.

4. Katie G. Cannon, *Black Womanist Ethics*, American Academy of Religion Series 60 (Atlanta: Scholars Press, 1988), 1–2.

5. Cannon, *Black Womanist Ethics*, 4.

6. Toinette M. Eugene, "Moral Values and Black Womanists," *Journal of Religious Thought* 44, no. 2 (1988): 33.

7. The literature on activism by black women in North America is prodigious, and includes issues such as their participation in the struggle for personal and group survival and in institutional transformation (including ecclesial, educational, economic, political, and local community institutions), their resiliency in the face of hardship and despair, their resistance to oppression, and their encounters with the multiple structures of oppression (gender, race, and class concerns).

William L. Andrews, *Sisters of the Spirit: Three Black Women's Autobiographies of the Nineteenth Century* (Bloomington: Indiana University Press, 1986).

Toni Cade (Bambara), "On the Issue of Roles," in *The Black Woman: An Anthology*, ed. Toni Cade (Bambara) (New York: Signet, 1970), 101–10.

Frances Beale, "Double Jeopardy: To Be Black and Female," in *The Black Woman: An Anthology*, ed. Toni Cade (Bambara) (New York: Signet, 1970), 90–100.

Evelyn Brooks, "The Feminist Theology of the Black Baptist Church, 1880–1900," in *Class, Race and Sex: The Dynamics of Control*, ed. Amy Swerdlow and Hanna Lessinger (Boston: G. K. Hall), 31–59.

Cynthia Stokes Brown, ed., *Ready from Within: Septima Clark and the Civil Rights Movement* (Navarro, Calif.: Wild Trees Press, 1986).

Alice Brown-Collins and Deborah Ridley Sussewell, "The Afro-American Women's Emerging Selves," *Journal of Black Psychology* 13, no. 1 (1986): 1–11.

Katie G. Cannon, "The Emergence of a Black Feminist Consciousness," in *Feminist Interpretations of the Bible*, ed. Letty M. Russell (Philadelphia: Westminster Press, 1985), 30–40.

Patricia Hill Collins, "The Afro-American Work Family Nexus: An Exploratory Analysis," *Western Journal of Black Studies* 10, no. 3 (1986): 148–58; "Learning from the Outsider Within: The Sociological Significance of Black Feminist Thought," *Social Problems* 33, no. 6 (1968): 14–32; "The Meaning of Motherhood in Black Culture and Black Mother/Daughter Relationships," *Sage* 4, no. 2 (1987): 4–11; "A Comparison of Two Works on Black Family Life," *Signs* 14, no. 4 (1989): 875–84.

R. Darcy and Charles D. Hadley, "Black Women in Politics: The Puzzle of Success," *Social Science Quarterly* 69, no. 3 (1988): 629–45.

Bonnie Thornton Dill, "The Dialectics of Black Womanhood," *Signs* 4, no. 3 (1979): 543–55; " 'The Means to Put My Children Through': Child-Rearing Goals and Strategies among Black Female Domestic Servants," in *The Black Women*, ed. La Frances Rodgers-Rose (Beverly Hills, Calif.: Sage, 1980), 107–23; "Race, Class, and Gender: Prospects for an All-Inclusive Sisterhood," *Feminist Studies* 9, no. 1 (1983): 131–50; " 'Making Your Job Good Yourself': Domestic Service and the Construction of Personal Dignity," in *Women and the Politics of Empowerment*, ed. Ann Bookman and Sandra Morgen (Philadelphia: Temple University Press, 1988), 33–52.

Rhetaugh Graves Dumas, "Dilemmas of Black Females in Leadership," in *The Black Woman*, ed. La Frances Rodgers-Rose (Beverly Hills, Calif.: Sage, 1980), 203–15.

Elizabeth Fox-Genovese, "Strategies and Forms of Resistance: Focus on Slave Women in the United States," in *In Resistance, Studies in African, Caribbean and Afro-American History*, ed. Gary Y. Okhiro (Amherst: University of Massachusetts Press, 1986), 143–65.

Cheryl Townsend Gilkes, " 'Holding Back the Ocean with a Broom': Black Women and Community Work," in *The Black Woman*, ed. La Frances Rodgers-Rose (Beverly Hills, Calif.: Sage, 1980), 217–32; "Successful Rebellious Professionals: The Black Woman's Professional Identity and Community Commitment," *Psychology of Women Quarterly* 6, no. 3 (1982): 289–311; "From Slavery to Social Welfare: Racism and the Control of Black Women," in *Class, Race, and Sex: The Dynamics of Control*, ed. Amy Swerdlow and Hanna Lessinger (Boston: G. K. Hall, 1983), 288–300; "Going Up for the Oppressed: The Career Mobility of Black Women Community Workers," *Journal of Social Issues* 39, no. 3 (1983): 115–39.

Evelyn Nakano Glenn, "Racial Ethnic Women's Labor: The Intersection of Race, Gender and Class Oppression," *Review of Radical Political Economics* 17, no. 3 (1985): 86–108.

Jacquelyn Grant, "Black Women and the Church," in *But Some of Us Are Brave*, ed. Gloria T. Hull, Patricia Bell Scott, and Barbara Smith (Old Westbury, N.Y.: Feminist Press, 1982), 141–52.

Beverly Guy-Sheftall, "Remembering Sojourner Truth: On Black Feminism," *Catalyst* (fall 1986): 54–57.

Sharon Harley, "Anna Julia Cooper: A Voice for Black Women," in *The Afro-American Women: Struggles and Images*, ed. Sharon Harley and Rosalyn Terborg-Penn (Port Washington, N.Y.: Kennikat Press, 1978), 87–96; "Beyond the Classroom: The Organizational Lives of Black Female Educators in the District of Columbia, 1890–1930," *Journal of Negro Education* 51, no. 3 (1982): 254–65; Sharon Harley and Rosalyn Terborg-Penn, eds., *The Afro-American Woman: Struggles and Images* (Port Washington, N.Y.: Kennikat Press, 1978).

Elizabeth Higginbotham, "Laid Bare by the System: Work and Survival for Black and Hispanic Woman," in *Class, Race, and Sex: The Dynamics of Control*, ed. Amy Swerdlow and Hanna Lessinger (Boston: G. K. Hall, 1983), 200–215.

Bell Hooks, *Ain't I a Woman: Black Women and Feminism* (Boston: South End Press, 1981).

Harriet Jacobs, "The Perils of a Slave Woman's Life," in *Invented Lives: Narratives of Black Women 1860–1960*, edited by Mary Helen Washington (Garden City, N.Y.: Anchor, 1987), 16–67.

Edward Mapp, "Black Women in Films," *Black Scholar* 4, no. 6–7 (1973): 42–46.

Manning Marable, "Grounding with My Sisters: Patriarchy and the Exploitation of Black Women," in *How Capitalism Underdeveloped Black America* (Boston: South End Press, 1983), 69–104.

Harriette Pipes McAdoo, "Strategies Used by Black Single Mothers against Stress," *Review of Black Political Economy* 14, no. 2–3 (1985): 153–66.

Cynthia Neverdon-Morton, *Afro-American Women of the South and the Advancement of the Race, 1895–1925* (Knoxville: University of Tennessee Press, 1989).

Jewell L. Prestage, "Political Behavior of American Black Women: An Overview," in *The Black Woman*, ed. La Frances Rodgers-Rose (Beverly Hills, Calif.: Sage, 1980), 233–50.

Bernice Johnson Reagon, "Coalition Politics: Turning the Century," in *Home Girls: A Black Feminist Anthology*, ed. Barbara Smith (New York: Kitchen Table Press, 1983), 356–68.

Marilyn Richardson, ed., *Maria W. Stewart, America's First Black Woman Political Writer* (Bloomington: Indiana University Press, 1987).

Karen Brodkin Sacks, "Computers, Ward Secretaries, and a Walkout in a Southern Hospital," in *My Troubles Are Going to Have Trouble with Me*, ed. Karen Sacks and Dorothy Remy (New Brunswick, N.J.: Rutgers University Press, 1984), 173–90.

Jean Reith Schroedel, *Alone in a Crowd: Women in the Trades Tell Their Stories* (Philadelphia: Temple University Press, 1985).

Rosalyn Terborg-Penn, "Discrimination against Afro-American Women in Woman's Movement, 1830–1920," in *The Afro-American Woman: Struggles and Images*, ed. Sharon Harley and Rosalyn Terborg-Penn (Port Washington, N.Y.: Kennikat Press, 1978), 17–27.

8. Jacquelyn Grant, "Black Theology and the Black Woman," in *Black Theology: A Documentary History, 1966–1979*, ed. Gayraud S. Wilmore and James H. Cone (Maryknoll, N.Y.: Orbis Books, 1979), 431.

9. For a review of the ways in which Jarena Lee, Sojourner Truth, and Francis Ellen Watkins Harper addressed the dual concerns of racism and sexism, see Rufus Burrow Jr., "Sexism in the Black Community and the Black Church," *Journal of the Interdenominational Theological Center*, no. 13 (1985–86): 317–32.

10. Bernice Johnson Reagon, "African Diaspora Women: The Making of Cultural Workers," in *Black Women's History: Theory and Practice*, vol. 2, ed. Darlene Clark Hine (Brooklyn: Carlson, 1990): 491–92.

11. Olive Gilbert, *Narrative of Sojourner Truth, with a History of Her Labors and Correspondence, Drawn from Her "Book of Life"* (Battle Creek, Mich., 1884).

12. Margaret Busby, ed., "Ann Plato," in *Daughters of Africa: An International Anthology of Words and Writings by Women of African Descent from the Ancient Egyptian to the Present* (New York: Pantheon, 1992), 75.

13. Ann Plato, *Essays: Including Biographies and Miscellaneous Pieces, in Prose and Poetry* (Hartford, 1841).

14. New Revised Standard Version, which is used for all Biblical citations in this essay.

15. George T. Montague, *Companion God: A Cross-Cultural Commentary on the Gospel of Matthew* (New York and Mahwah, N.J.: Paulist Press, 1989), 160.

16. On the formation of pearls, see Frederick H. Pough, "pearl," *World Book Encyclopedia*, vol. 15 (Chicago: Field Enterprises Educational Corporation, 1964), 193. Note in particular the discussion of how the foreign irritant is transformed into a lustrous pearl by the nacre (the liquid substance lining the shell).

17. I am not valorizing racial struggle or suffering as laudable and potentially redemptive because it yields something of great value. Oppression is a result of sin's effects in a fallen world, a form of injustice and evil, and it thwarts God's liberating and loving purposes for humanity. I am affirming and applauding the stream and tradition of black women's wisdom, resiliency, perseverance, and perceptivity that emerged in the midst of and in spite of struggle and adversity.

18. Walter E. Fluker, *The National Resource Center for Ethical Leadership*

Handbook (Colgate Rochester Divinity School, Rochester, N.Y., 17 March 1992), 5, app. 4, 1.

19. There are numerous examples. See, for example, Bradford Chambers, *Chronicle of Black Protest* (New York: New American Library, 1968). In a major section entitled "Let No Man Hold Back" (153–244), *all* persons cited as making significant and salient efforts to advance the cause of civil rights are black males: Booker T. Washington, A. Philip Randolph, Martin Luther King Jr., and Malcolm X.

20. For a helpful survey of the evolution of definitions of leadership from the 1900s to the 1990s, with a discussion of the problems with defining "leadership" in the literature, see Joseph C. Rost, *Leadership for the Twenty-first Century* (New York: Praeger, 1991), especially 36–65. Rost's review of definitions of leadership in the years 1900–79 in English dictionaries reveals some of the complexities that arise in conceptualizing and practicing leadership. First, "leadership" did not come into regular usage until the turn of the century, and even then, it did not convey the popular connotations that persons attach to it today. Second, it is not the case that the modern concept of leadership has been in use since Greco-Roman antiquity; it is fully a twentieth-century concept. The word "leader" even had different connotations in the seventeenth century than it does in the twentieth century, due, in part, to the democratization of Western civilization. Third, dictionary definitions of leadership in the years 1900–79 are simply not helpful in understanding the concept, nor do they account for the complexity of the concept as it is revealed in books and journal articles on leadership — perhaps a function of its ambiguity in popular discourse and its lack of precise definition in scholarly literature. Fourth, dictionaries have tended to employ "leadership" and "management" as synonymous terms, so that leadership is defined as "holding the position or office of a leader." Administrative or management functions are in view. Fifth, dictionaries tend to equate leadership with certain identifiable "traits." Moreover, and perhaps more importantly, they tend to suggest that leadership resides almost solely in the leader, rather than involving a relationship between and among leaders' followers.

21. Nathan Irvin Huggins, "Afro-Americans," in *Ethnic Leadership in America*, ed. John Higham (Baltimore: Johns Hopkins University Press, 1978), 93.

22. Huggins, "Afro-Americans," 93.

23. Reviews of the scientific treatment of female leadership, including concepts and theories, are conspicuously lacking until the late 1970s. Prior to this time, most leadership research was carried out by men and dealt exclusively with male subjects. Analyses of the conceptual status of gender in the literature (Do women and men differ as leaders? How do gender stereotypes affect the perception, description, and evaluation of women in leadership positions?) have proliferated since the late 1970s. See Lenelis Kruse and Margret Wintermantel, "Leadership Ms.-Qualified I: The Gender Bias in Everyday Scientific Thinking," and Erika Apfelbaum and Martha Hadley, "Leadership Ms.-Qualified II: Reflections on an Initial Case Study Investigation of Contemporary Women Leaders," in *Changing Concepts of Leadership*, ed. Carl F. Graumann and Serge Moscovici

(New York: Springer-Verlag, 1986), 171–221; Bernard M. Bass, "Women and Leadership," in *Stogdill's Handbook of Leadership: A Survey of Theory and Research*, rev. ed. (New York: Free Press, 1981), 491–507.

24. Thomas Rose and John Greenya, *Black Leaders Then and Now: A Personal History of Students Who Led the Civil Rights Movement in the 1960s — And What Happened to Them* (Garrett Park, Md.: Garrett Park Press, 1984).

25. Barbara Reynolds, *And Still We Rise: Interviews with 50 Black Role Models* (Washington, D.C.: Gannett, 1988).

26. Columbus Salley, *The Black 100: A Ranking of the Most Influential African Americans, Past and Present* (New York: Carol Publishing Group, 1993), xiii. A total of 102 black influentials results from three pairs being listed and ranked as one (see the discussion on page xiv).

27. Alice Walker, *In Search of Our Mothers' Gardens* (New York: Harcourt, Brace, Jovanovich, 1983), xi. See the works of Katie G. Cannon, *Black Womanist Ethics*, American Academy of Religion Series 60 (Atlanta: Scholars Press, 1988); Toinette M. Eugene, "Moral Values and Black Womanists," *Journal of Religious Thought* 44 (winter–spring 1988): 23–34; Jacqueline Grant, "Womanist Theology: Black Women's Experience as a Source for Doing Theology, with Special Reference to Christology," *Journal of the Interdenominational Theological Center* 13, no. 2 (spring 1986): 195–212; Renita J. Weems, *Just a Sister Away: A Womanist Vision of Women's Relationships in the Bible* (San Diego: LuraMedia, 1988); Delores S. Williams, "Womanist Theology: Black Women's Voices," *Christianity and Crisis* 47 (2 March 1987): 66–70. For a fuller listing of womanist scholarship, see the helpful essay by womanist theologian Kelly D. Brown, "God Is As Christ Does: Toward a Womanist Theology," *Journal of Religious Thought* 46, no. 1 (summer–fall 1989), 7–16. See also, Clarice J. Martin, "Womanist Interpretations of the New Testament: The Quest for Holistic and Inclusive Translation and Interpretation," *Journal of Feminist Studies in Religion* 6, no. 2 (1990): 41–61.

28. Fluker, *Ethical Leadership Handbook*, 7.

29. Ethicists Katie Cannon and Emilie Townes set about this task in their respective works, *Black Womanist Ethics*, American Academy of Religion Series 60 (Atlanta: Scholars Press, 1988), and *Womanist Justice, Womanist Hope*, American Academy of Religion Series 79 (Atlanta: Scholars Press, 1993). Cannon studies the writings of Zora Neale Hurston; Townes focuses on Ida B. Wells Barnett. Also see theologian Delores S. Williams's essay on the nature of black women's experience as it is inscribed in three twentieth-century novels: Margaret Walker's *Jubliee*, Zora Neale Hurston's *Jonah's Gourd Vine*, and Alice Walker's *The Color Purple* ("Black Women's Literature and the Task of Feminist Theology," in *Immaculate and Powerful: The Female in Sacred Image and Social Reality*, ed. Clarissa W. Atkinson, Constance H. Buchanan, and Margaret R. Miles [Boston: Beacon, 1985], 88–110). These and other womanist religion scholars document the importance of the black woman's literary tradition as a resource for the moral and ethical development of black women and black peoples.

30. Eugene, "Moral Values and Black Womanists," 33.

31. Eugene, "Moral Values and Black Womanists," 33.

32. Clarice J. Martin, "Biblical Theodicy and Black Women's Spiritual Auto-biography: 'The Miry Bog, the Desolate Pit, a New Song in my Mouth,'" in *A Troubling in My Soul: Womanist Perspectives on Evil and Suffering*, ed. Emilie M. Townes (Maryknoll, N.Y.: Orbis Books, 1993), 30–31.

33. See the full citation of Stewart's statement at the opening of this essay.

34. See note 1 for the publishing information on Stewart's *Productions*.

35. For a more extensive discussion of the nature and function of nineteenth-century black women's spiritual autobiographies, see Clarice J. Martin, "Biblical Theodicy," 13–36.

36. Stewart, *Productions*, 1–2.

37. Stewart, *Productions*, 4. See also Marilyn Richardson, *Maria W. Stewart, America's First Black Woman Political Writer: Essays and Speeches* (Bloomington and Indianapolis: Indiana University Press, 1987).

38. Stewart, *Productions*, 15. Refer back to the quotation that opens this essay.

39. Dennis R. Bratcher, "rush," *Harper's Bible Dictionary*, ed. Paul J. Achtemeier (San Francisco: Harper and Row, 1985), 885–86.

40. Stewart, *Productions*, 12.

41. Bernhard W. Anderson, *Understanding the Old Testament*, 4th ed. (Englewood Cliffs, N.J.: Prentice-Hall, 1986), 310.

42. Wolfgang Schrage, *The Ethics of the New Testament*, trans. David E. Green (Philadelphia: Fortress, 1988), 40–43.

43. Schrage, *Ethics*, 187–88.

44. Stewart, *Productions*, 5–7.

45. Stewart, *Productions*, 11, 13.

46. Leslie J. Hoppe, *Being Poor: A Biblical Study*, Good News Studies, 20 (Wilmington, Del.: Michael Glazier, 1987), 5–9.

47. Philip Francis Esler, *Community and Gospel in Luke-Acts: The Social and Political Motivations of Lucan Theology* (New York: Cambridge University Press, 1987), 193.

48. Stewart, *Productions*, 4–5.

49. Gayraud S. Wilmore, *Black Religion and Black Radicalism*, 2d ed. (Maryknoll, N.Y.: Orbis Books, 1989), 239–40.

50. Stewart, *Productions*, 15–16.

51. Stewart, *Productions*, 16–17.

5

Keeping Faith with the People
Reflections on Ethics, Leadership, and
African-American Women's Historical Experience
CHERYL TOWNSEND GILKES

*Hatreds never cease by hatreds in this world. By love alone they cease.
This is an ancient law.*[1]

Perhaps the quintessential example of African-American leadership
rooted in the ethical traditions of the black church tradition was the
woman or man who first sang during slavery, perhaps in a hush harbor
meeting, "I've got a right, you've got a right, we've all got a right to the
tree of life." From within the belly of the beast of slavery came a voice
stating, in the clear and unequivocal way that singers always do, that
not only were there universal human claims to life, but also that life was
symbolized in the form of a tree that stood closest to the sources and
seat of God's power. Not only did this "black and unknown bard" assert
the humanity of the singer and her or his hearers in an institutional and
cultural matrix organized for the total negation of African-American
humanity, but she or he exercised a form of leadership that placed healing and wholeness as integral elements of the moral claims of being.
The raising of a voice with images of life, health, wholeness, and healing is perhaps the most elemental form of ethical leadership rooted in
black church tradition.

The process of thinking of ethics and African-American leadership
comes at a moment in African-American life and culture when one
of the most destructive crises in self-esteem and being currently rages.
And I choose the word "rages" quite purposefully. Everywhere we turn,
we see evidence of African-American rage turned in on itself. In popular culture, particularly, it is evident in the various forms of rap music.
In some of this music, for instance a piece by Snoop Doggy Dog, black
men and women actually take the form of dogs to express the essence of
their beings. (When I pointed this problem out to some young people

from my church one night, they turned around and said, "Well, what about those 'Q-dogs'?") Another form of rap music, "gangsta rap," finds women and men reducing each other to their various body parts. Ironically, the lucrativeness of the market for this music is heavily fueled by white people who find pleasure in these images of black self-destruction and rage. This rage is also evident in the alternative system of income production — the drug industry — that has produced well-organized armies of men, mostly, whose predatory discipline produces death after death after death.

As one moves across the dimensions of African-American experience and history, from the hush harbor to the impoverished urban ghetto, it is clear that African Americans have always been entangled in the throes of cultural warfare. Although our reason for being there was primarily the economic exploitation at the root of American racism, and although the maintenance of our subordination in this society has been largely the efforts of well-organized and efficient political action, the cultural denigration of African Americans has been instrumental and key in maintaining our "living death" in this society. In so many ways, the society has sought to annihilate our humanity.

Some of the most glaring failures of leadership in the African-American experience have been the failures of those in key positions within and outside the community to actively resist the cultural dimensions of our annihilation in a racist society. From the vantage point of the late twentieth century, the suppressed singing voices of our ancestors seem so much clearer and more forceful than the diverse, qualified voices that are beamed to us through CNN. Although appearances can be deceiving, the themes and the struggles and the strengths from the distant past seem to stand before us more clearly in terms of mission and community resolve.

Seeking to explore the connection between past themes and present emergencies, this essay focuses on several dimensions or domains of ethical leadership in order to sketch areas of concern and inquiry for the development of "ethical leadership" for the contemporary African-American community. There is one key point in the essay: African-American women's organizational, political, and cultural history contains important practical and theoretical resources for defining and interpreting models of leadership. This essay draws on diverse sources for its reflections on this point. First of all, it is informed by research conducted in a northeast, urban, African-American community on women who were perceived by members of the community to be leaders; they were perceived as leaders by virtue of their being identified as having "worked hard for a long time for change in the black community."[2] The essay is also informed by the historical connections drawn between these women and a larger historical tradition of women's work for social change and community survival. The women's role models and their sense of mission were derived not only from their religious and political experiences as young people in African-American communities, but, once their lives became entwined with the public struggles of African Americans, they also connected across generations of women engaged in similar activities and connected with the tradition of social action in a very real way. In addition to these women, related work focused on women in religious institutions provides a resource for insights on ethical leadership.[3] All of this connects with various theoretical voices concerning the roles of African-American women, from Alice Walker and her idea/ideal of "womanist" to Patricia Hill Collins and her discussions of the "recurring humanist vision" in the organizational history of African-American women and their teaching role as the "outsider within" an oppressive society.[4] In reflecting on the problem of "ethical leadership," then, this essay wanders through a broad range of empirical and reflective experiences. It is not a scholarly piece, but seeks to learn from my own professional and reflective experience in order to point to directions of purpose for future leaders. Most of all, I hope to show that the traditions of leadership found in African-American women's experience offer models for women and men, and provide an accurate reflection of the range of problems facing African Americans in the United States. A starting point for these models of leadership can be found in African-American women's experience, an experience that involves persistence at keeping faith with African-American people.

African-American Women
and Traditions of Leadership

The importance of African-American women, their history and experience, to reflections on leadership has to be argued. This is a racist and a sexist society, and part of the history of African Americans is tied directly to an assault organized with reference to gender. While the "ideals of womanhood" were negated during slavery in order to extract as much as possible from women as beasts of burden, African Americans were simultaneously culturally denigrated, labeled, or deviantized because of the strength cultivated among women as they survived the demands on them as workers, mothers, wives, family members, and responsible community builders.[5] Indeed the racialized sexism of the United States imposed a deficit model on the African-American community that attempted to explain the seemingly great strength of women as a response to the weakness and emasculation of men. The stereotype of "Mammy," the large, overbearing, take-charge, extremely religious woman, was inextricably lined to the childlike, weak, and ineffectual "Sambo." The stereotype of Mammy, one of several vicious distortions of African-American women's history, is so strong that it spills over into the expectations placed on African-American women in the contemporary professional, business, and academic settings of white America.

I would like to think that the singer whom I mentioned was a woman. Several resources on life in the slave community hint that such a presupposition would not be off target. Women and men who left records of their experiences as slaves point to the voices of their mothers as those that provided the "cultural scripts" of inner or spiritual strength. The song and the prayer were sources of strength in a world that was wearying in its oppression. So many of the spirituals, when speaking of the singer, speak of the personal consequences of the oppressive experience, and the earliest voices offering leadership are those of the preacher, the song leader, and the prayer warrior. Both fictional and historical narratives point to the voices of women in this chorus of strength. In a very moving passage in Beloved, Toni Morrison sketches a portrait of the evangelist Baby Suggs as she preaches to men, women, and children to love themselves because the world beyond the community hates them. She insists that this love is oppositional because the world seeks to kill and destroy black flesh.

In a sense, the songs and prayers of slavery contain the paradigm of leadership that emerges from African-American women's activities. Historians who have bothered to pay attention to women in the slave community have cited the communalism among these women and their role in nurturing the two institutions that promoted the survival and asserted the humanity of enslaved women and men: religion and the family. In both the invisible and visible manifestations of the religious life, women are prominent and work to promote continuity. In addition to spiritual leadership, women are documented as healers and teachers. Those who learned to read taught others — one critical example being Milla Granson, a Kentucky slave woman who ran a clandestine school teaching twelve disciples at a time. Mamie Garvin Fields, in her memoir, describes ancestors — women and men — who, once they acquired literacy, passed it on. Ellen Craft, a literate woman light enough to pass, wrote papers for her husband to accompany her as her body servant while she disguised herself as a man on their near-legendary escape to freedom. William and Ellen Craft, powerful antislavery workers, returned to the South after freedom to teach.

Example after example can be marshaled of women nurturing the community's sense of itself as a spiritually obligated collection of people responsible for each other's wholeness, health, and healing — a group of people in a shared situation with "a right to the tree of life." Included in that sense is a commitment to the education of one another — the sharing of knowledge that fostered and enabled survival. The education of the community in clandestine and public settings is a theme that is one of the largest brush strokes of African-American history and, according to Du Bois's observations, this history is heavily a women's history.

During slavery, other traditions of leadership emerged in the free black communities of the North. Here women participated in the founding of churches. They formed mutual aid and benevolent societies within churches and outside of them. In addition to nurturing survival through cooperative economics and benevolence, they also formed their own antislavery societies to advance the cause of abolition. Various individual leaders gained prominence, and their prominence was tied to their exhortation to women to move beyond the domestic sphere and take seriously the importance of their leadership. Maria Stewart, the first woman of any color to lecture publicly and leave a legacy of manuscripts, was particularly passionate in urging the daughters of Africa to take their rightful place in a heroic history of women who made a difference in the world. Women in free black communities made such outstanding contributions that whites noted the difference in the observations of women's public roles, and black men sometimes took the lead in removing formal barriers to women's participation.

The rise of Jim Crow prompted many responses from African-American women. Ironically, the most prominent organized response came in the form of the anti-lynching movement. Ida B. Wells-Barnett's anti-lynching crusade became an occasion for organized support by women. They had no problem recognizing the integral relationship between the vicious mob assaults on black men and the racist ideological matrix that offered distorted images of male and female sexuality. The movement that emerged from the women's meetings in Boston, New York, and Washington, D.C. focused on a broad range of issues that not only spoke to the needs of both women and men, but also defined the principal problems confronting the black community in terms of the futures of their children.

This focus on children and their future has been present in every organized expression of African-American women's activism. In oral histories I collected and in autobiographies I have surveyed, there can be observed at least three bases on which women act in ways that eventually lead to their public leadership. Although women may be moved to address conditions confronting them as women or conditions confronting the men in their lives, they most often come to public action on issues concerning children. It is important not to read this as a relegation of children's issues to the women's sphere, but rather, given the history of the legal struggles surrounding Jim Crow, as evidence of the centrality of the assault on black children to the operation of racial oppression in America.

The organized life of African-American women and their leaders points to the centrality of the spiritual in definitions of leadership and themes of action. Not only in religious and fraternal groups, but also in ostensibly secular activities, for instance the National Council of Negro Women, the religious dimensions of African-American life are woven into political and organizational ideologies. This is a dimension of ethical leadership that must be taken seriously.

The Lessons of Women's History

Reviewing the different historical periods of the African-American experience points to the persistence with which women contributed leadership and energy to resolving the diverse problems African-American people have faced. My own observations of community workers, church women, and some of the directions signaled by the work of historians such as Deborah Gray White and Evelyn Brooks Higginbotham indicate that any historical analysis of leadership must be revisionist in terms of centering women's experience in that analysis. Many perspectives on the African-American experience have either blotted out the contributions of women or assumed that these women were wrong in their persistence at public participation. These assumptions, I believe, have distorted the work of people like E. Franklin Frazier. Indeed I think some of this work needs to be re-read as a defense of a patriarchy that he presumed to be the dominant culture norm to which African Americans should assimilate.

One of the first lessons to be taken from women's leadership styles and practice is the resistance to disconnection that seems to be part of the African-American women's experience. That resistance to disconnection is captured in Alice Walker's insistence that the ethical ideal for black women is "not separatist, except periodically, for health."[6] There is an ethic among black women community workers that evinces an insistence on "being there" as an important stance for social change. Women sometimes emphasize a presence in critical settings or sites rather than actually heading organizations or controlling spaces. There can be a greater concern for the dynamics of organizational culture than with issues of authority.

When African-American women have felt blocked from contributing their visions for leadership in religious and secular settings, their organizational challenges have been explicit in their inclusion of men. This is true in both religious and secular settings. It is rare for women to openly reject male leadership and participation.[7] Rather, they will form their own organizations and then invite men into their space. The women's club movement of the late nineteenth and early twentieth centuries was quite explicit in its rejection of separatism. "We are neither alienating nor withdrawing," declared Josephine St. Pierre Ruffin. She indicated that black women were simply taking their rightful places at the front, as leaders, "for the benefit of women and men." She then indicated that men were invited to join.

One particularly important example of this resistance to disconnection can be found in Frances Ellen Watkins Harper's *Iola Leroy,* a novel that offers an African-American woman's perspective on leadership, ethics, and connection during and after slavery. Harper defines being black as a conscious choice and commitment to keeping faith with a people who share suffering at the same time they share diverse approaches to ameliorating that suffering. Throughout the novel she points to the importance of consciously joining with African Americans — in a voice that parallels James Baldwin's insistence that race and racial identity are moral choices — in a struggle to assert humanity, to reconstruct community, and to seek social justice.[8]

A second lesson from women's history is the importance of the cultural dimension in defining and shaping the manner in which issues of social change are addressed and the images of self that are projected in activist settings. Racial oppression in its most simplistic description is at least a threefold process of domination: economic, political, and cultural. The history of racial domination is tied to a history of gendered images and interpretations of the black experience that have served to argue and reinforce in the public mind notions of black inferiority. African-American women have made some of their most militant eruptions around the issue of denigration of women. Long ago, Anna Julia Cooper asserted that the continued denigration of African Americans was very much tied to the position and perception of women in the society. Alice Walker once wrote that the world should have declared a public emergency on the day that a black woman complained that the collard greens purchased in the local supermarket tasted like dishwater, because underneath that complaint was the evidence of ecological disaster. In the same way, we must see Anna Julia Cooper's observation, which stated that only when the dignity of African-American women is upheld in all settings of American life can the dignity and humanity of all African Americans be sustained, as evidence of the cultural disaster that undergirds American racism. We must take seriously her perception, and approach far more critically and militantly those dimensions of culture that reinforce the exploitation and domination in the economic and political spheres.

A third, but not final, lesson coming from women's history is the lesson of collective discipline. In our rush to focus primarily on the blocked access of women to pulpits, and an axiomatic focus on women's resistance to women preachers, we have ignored the traditions of organized life among church women. These women exercise an amazing collective discipline. When once asked to discuss the resistance of women to women's leadership, I had to point out before answering the question that when we look only at the seeming resistance of women to women preachers, we ignore a tremendous leadership history among organized African-American women. My own research on leaders in an urban community discerned patterns that were borne out at the national level: when African-American women achieve leadership positions in male dominated political settings, that achievement is usually engineered through women's organizational settings. W. E. B. Du Bois complained much about the fractiousness of black men, and posited that the "intellectual leadership of the race" was perhaps in the hands of African-American women. While not claiming the superiority of women, Du Bois was reflecting on his observations of their organizational discipline.

In all of our deliberations on the nature of leadership and the ethical content of the appropriate leadership styles and ideologies, it is important to take seriously the integration of women's history, experience, and voices. African-American women have a complex and vibrant history of shaping cultural agency within the African-American experience. Given the overt sexist resistance to their leadership and participation in many settings in the black community and the current misogynist discourse of contemporary popular culture, there are values within this world of women that bear exploring. The emerging historical theme is that the women who care to be activist have persisted in believing in the collective possibilities of African Americans and have fostered, at some times and in some conditions, an ideal that has kept them, in the words of Alice Walker, "committed to survival and wholeness of entire people, male *and* female." At the root of any idea of ethical leadership is the understanding that the kinds of leaders needed by African Americans are those able to "keep faith with the people." African-American women's history needs to be at the center of an analysis that will enhance this process of keeping faith.

Notes

1. Bukkyo Dendo Kyokai, *The Teaching of Buddha* (Tokyo: Bukkyo Dendo Kyokai, 1966).

2. The entire study is available in my dissertation, "Living and Working in a World of Trouble: The Emergent Career of the Black Woman Community Worker," Ph.D. diss., Northeastern University, 1979.

3. See Cheryl Townsend Gilkes, "The Role of Women in the Sanctified Church," *Journal of Religious Thought* 43, no. 1: 24–41; and "The Roles of Church and Community Mothers: Ambivalent American Sexism or Fragmented African Familyhood?" *Journal of Feminist Studies in Religion* 2 (Spring): 41–59.

4. See Alice Walker, "Womanist," *In Search of our Mothers' Gardens: Womanist Prose* (New York: Harcourt Brace Jovanovich, 1983), xi–xii, especially her dictionary-style definition of "womanist" at the beginning of the book; and Patricia Hill Collins, *Black Feminist Thought: Knowledge, Consciousness, and the Politics of Empowerment* (Cambridge, Mass.: Unwin Hyman, 1990).

5. Important perspectives relevant here can be found in Angela Davis's classic essay on the role of African-American women in the community of slaves, in *Women, Race, and Class* (New York: Random House, 1981), and in Deborah Gray White's discussion of the female slave network in her book *Ar'n't I a Woman: Female Slaves in the Plantation South* (New York: W. W. Norton and Company, 1985).

6. Walker, *Our Mothers' Gardens*, xi.

7. This resistance to separatism has been observed even in the most explicitly and militantly feminist dimensions among African-American women, for instance the Combahee River Statement, reprinted in several places, and cited by ethicist Barbara Hilkert Andolsen in *"Daughters of Jefferson, Daughters of Bootblacks": Racism and American Feminism* (Macon, Ga.: Mercer University Press, 1986). She points out that male-female cooperation is one of the greatest areas of disagreement between black and white feminists.

8. James Baldwin, "On Being White and Other Lies," *Essence*, April 1984, 90–94.

6

Retrieving and Reappropriating the Values of the Black Church Tradition through Written Narratives

CAROLYN C. DENARD

Introduction

If what we mean when we refer to the values of the black church tradition are those moral and ethical values that sustained the African-American community throughout its journey in the Americas, and whose administrative locus was the black church, then we are speaking mostly of values that were born and actualized during the period of cohesive African-American community life that thrived during the era of segregation. The black church tradition, as opposed to church tradition or white church tradition, was born out of an effort to interpret the ethical and moral mission of African Americans in terms that would meet the challenges they faced in this world as oppressed and dispossessed people — the values they used to maintain their dignity, their humanity, and their faith in God during a time when they were not respected and treated as human in the larger society. Such values, while largely taught, upheld and encouraged by the black church, also extended beyond the black church and were shared by the black secular community as well. My understanding of the black church tradition, then, as it relates to ethical values, is a tradition that extended beyond the church itself, and included the secular ethical community as well. I will refer to this tradition, not antithetically but more encompassingly, as the black ethical tradition.

The morals and values of this tradition shaped generations of African Americans, and the leaders who became representative of these values are exemplary. These leaders — King, Thurman, Watson, Du Bois, Washington, Bethune, and others — were able to advance this tradition of values and draw on it in their time of need. It was not only a code to live by but also a balm for the racist restrictions they faced in the larger society. There is much to be learned from the transformative and healing possibilities of such a tradition. It saved a people from destruction. It taught them the values of community love and Godly purpose, of individual respect and accountability, the value of an honored life of principle and good character rather than a famed life of good fortune. The instructive and transformative possibilities of lives guided by such a tradition are great, and we should be eager to appropriate the lessons of these ways of living in our contemporary lives.

The difficulty, however, in maintaining the vitality of this tradition and especially of using it as a model for ethical leadership in the contemporary period is in *accessing* those values with the same kind of immediacy and relevance as those who grew up during the making of this tradition were able to do. With the end of segregation, the variables that had made the distinctive black ethical tradition vital and immediate were changed. Integration and the cultural revolution of the 1960s altered the distinctive shape and, in some cases, the "felt need" for that tradition, and made the living ethical tradition, of which we speak and wish to evoke, a tradition linked to a specific, past historical context. To seek to access these values now — self-consciously and for their heuristic value — from a context where the tradition was accessed daily, subconsciously, and experientially, is a difficult undertaking. And so one of our major tasks now as we try to draw from the values of that tradition is deciding how we can viably transmit those values when the context under which they were born and sustained no longer exists. How do we retrieve in the present those values of the past, isolate them from context, and name them so that we can, to the extent possible, reappropriate them?

The time prior to integration, when the values of the black ethical tradition were practiced and exercised daily by most blacks, we must accept now as a time of memory. That does not diminish the reappropriative potential of this tradition, but it does affect how we invoke it and cull from it what was valuable. We must depend on memory — written and oral — to re-create and invoke that time. We must create what French historian Pierre Nora calls "sites of memory," places where memory "crystallizes and secrets itself." Such sites become necessary, Nora explains, when "the remnants of experience still lived in the warmth of tradition, in the silence of custom, in the repetition of the ancestral, have been displaced under the pressure of a fundamentally historical sensibility."[1] We now live in such a time, and thus we must identify and construct "sites of memory" to serve as the resource places where we preserve the values of the black ethical tradition in context as best we can. These places of memory will become the sites we mine, again and again, as we seek to extract those ethical values that we believe will be instructive models for living in contemporary society.

Proposal

I wish to suggest in this paper that written narratives — remembered imaginative stories (novels) and remembered personal narratives (auto-biographies) — can serve as useful sites of memory that we may use in our goal of retrieving and reappropriating the values of the black church tradition. Remembered narratives — imagined and real — of the life contexts of a time now past can function as ethnographic descriptions of that time past. They can become, in the absence of the lived life of that time, the "cultural scripts" that we can use in the present to see how these values functioned in their original, albeit remembered, con-texts. Through proper cultural analysis of these "scripts," we can begin to isolate and name those values that were part of the black ethical tra-dition and offer them as exemplary models for how we might live more ethically grounded lives today.

There are many reasons why narratives can be helpful in this re-trieval and reappropriation of the values of this tradition. I will outline those reasons here, and then offer practical ways of implementing these analyses in seminars and training sessions where we seek to teach and reappropriate the moral and ethical life of traditional African-American communities.

At the outset, however, I think a word or two must be said about the validity of using imaginative narratives in this retrieval. The valid-ity of using imaginative narratives is grounded in my belief in a *cognitive* definition of culture. According to cognitive theorists in cultural an-thropology, culture is a knowledge system existing in people's minds that they use to govern behavior.[2] It is not the behavior itself that con-stitutes culture, but the cognitive systems of ideas, values, and beliefs that people must know in order to *generate* behavior acceptable to the cultural group. Although imaginative stories are not "factual" or "real" in the way that the personal history narratives of autobiography are, imaginative narratives can be culturally valid. If the values the writer uses to govern the behavior of the imagined characters in the text are real, then it does not matter, in this cognitive view of culture, whether the behavior is real or not. What *is* important is that the values govern-ing even this fictional, created behavior within an imagined narrative be true to the values in the real cultural community operating outside the novel and on which the novel is based. It is not documentable behavior that we are after ultimately in cultural analysis, but the belief systems of values and ideas that govern that behavior.

The potential for imaginative stories to serve as exemplars of moral and ethical life has been assumed for centuries by literary scholars, as evidenced by the perennial offerings in the humanities of courses devoted to "literary classics." In these courses, the goal is not the appreciation, necessarily, of the period of the craft of the literature, but the lessons of life these "great books" are believed to offer to each generation of students. The most recent and popular demonstration of this assumption outside of the humanities has been advanced by Robert Coles, who uses what he calls the moral imagination embedded in stories — classic and contemporary — to teach ethics to students of law and medicine.[3] Even more recently, former Secretary of Education William Bennett has employed this same function of imagined stories in his collection of moral stories called *The Book of Virtues*.[4] In this collection, Bennett compiles a cornucopia of stories that show by example moral and ethical values to live by.

Finally, and perhaps most importantly for our purposes, there now exists a generation of African-American writers who, socialized in the segregated communities of the past and affected by the ethical void they see in the present culture, are using their imaginative stories as ways to reconnect with the ethical tradition that we wish to retrieve. Their goal in writing these stories is to mine and preserve those values. "There has to be a mode," explains Toni Morrison, "to do what the music did for blacks, what we used to be able to do with each other. . . . I think long and carefully about what my novels ought to do. They should clarify the roles that have become obscured; they ought to identify those things in the past that are useful and those things that are not; and they ought to give nourishment."[5] Writer John Wideman echoes that sentiment: "In the writing that I have been doing for the last three or four years, I have been trying to recover some of that lost experience, to re-educate myself about some of the things I missed because the world was moving so fast. I am trying to listen again . . . [and] books were a way of returning."[6] If we were to dismiss imaginative narratives because they are not "factual accounts" of lives lived or because they were not "true," then we would miss the enormous contribution these works can make to the ethical mission we seek to achieve. To omit such works where the expressed intent is *to retrieve* would cut scholars off from an expressive and insightful group of informants whose imaginative stories can provide valuable resources for both retrieving and reappropriating the cultural life of the past.

Having established the theoretical base for the use of imaginative narratives in retrieving values of a real cultural past and the precedents in using imaginative texts in this way, I outline now what I believe to be the practical and functional values of using narratives as vehicles through which we access aspects of the black ethical tradition.

The Benefits of Using Narratives in Retrieval and Reappropriation of Ethical Values

1. Accessible Mode of Comprehension

Narratives — novels, short stories, and autobiographies — are valuable in the service of reappropriation, first of all, because they make specific use of narrative form, which is the most basic form of comprehension, or, as Robert Coles puts it, "everybody's rock-bottom capacity and universal gift."[7] It is through the act of constructing narratives that we come to understand cognitively what we know about the world. Narratives help us to order the complexity of our own experience and the experience of others. As psychologist Barbara Hardy has explained, "We dream in narrative, daydream in narrative, remember, anticipate, hope, despair, believe, doubt, plan, revise, criticize, construct, gossip, learn, hate, and love by narrative."[8] Narrative is a way of taking all the random events in life and giving them order and purpose. It is the way, quite simply, that we make sense of our lives. Narratives are, as Louis Mink concludes, "primary and irreducible. They are not imperfect substitutes for more sophisticated forms of explanation and understanding, nor are they unreflective first steps along the road which lead toward the goal of scientific or philosophical knowledge. The comprehension at which stories aim is a primary act of mind."[9] Stories aid in that comprehension by constructing and relating the events to each other. Stories provide starting points and ending points, articulation and conflict, themes, and resolution. Thus, when we seek to revisit a time past, when we seek to make sense of experience and give comprehensible order to the experience of the past — whether through song or poetry, through wise grandmothers or streetcorner griots — the most effective way of communicating and explaining the life of the past has always been to tell a story. "I don't understand," says the novice or outsider. "Let me tell you a story," answers the elder or insider. It is a pattern as old as language itself. In form alone, then, imaginative narratives — unlike statistical reports of journalistic newsreels, or historical documentation — offer a natural means of accessing and bringing order to the culture of the past.

2. Continuous Historical Present

Imaginative narratives, particularly, are also important in the service of reappropriating the past because they offer an opportunity to enter into that past as if in a present moment, or in what literary critics call "the continuous historical present."[10] Part of the problem with those who wish to retrieve the values of the past by returning physically to the old communities has been the often disappointing realization that they — to borrow Thomas Wolfe's lament — really "can't go home again," at least not in the same way as they left home behind. The home of the actual present is never the same as it is remembered to be. The people, the organization of the community, the setting, the smells, the way language is used, the way news is passed on, is never — with the forward movement of history — the same as it is remembered. The presently experienced moment of a remembered time or place may be sweet, it may be loving, it may be peaceful and welcoming, but it never offers exactly the same social and cultural context and situational nuance of the time now gone. The going back always happens with the frustrating realization that the ethos that one searches for must be modified or adjusted — talked about but not exactly experienced — for the present time. Quite literally in many cases — to use Professor Fluker's eloquent metaphor — "the ground has shifted" in these communities, and the context and meaning of life and the ebb and flow of the land are no longer constituted as they once were.[11]

For an understanding of past time to have its greatest value, ideally it must be seen as it *was*. Through the skillful use of language combined with a knowledge of history, geography, architecture, and culture, the fiction writer can re-create the past with all the nuances of language, dress, colors, smells, sights, emotions, ideas, and terrain just as they were. In imaginative fiction, in other words, *the ground does not shift*. The values and ideas that one is seeking to recover and that are irretrievable in actual physical returns can be re-created in imaginative fiction.

When we pick up a novel, it is always present. When Hester Prynne leaves the prison of Massachusetts Bay in *The Scarlet Letter,* she always leaves on the day that the reader opens the novel for the first time. When Robert Smith leaps from the top of Mercy Hospital in Toni Morrison's *Song of Solomon,* it is always February 18, 1931. It is always winter, the red rose petals are always scattered vividly against the snow, Pilate's contralto is always just as compelling. The reader enters into the fiction, and every action there follows the time and terrain of the story's creation. Readers move from February 18, 1931 through twenty years of Milkman's life, but the reader begins at the same moment each time the novel is read. The story of the past is always happening "now."

Anthropologist Eric Lardel has explained the "always present" value of the narrative in his discussion of mythic narratives. His explanation, while referring to the mythic, the ancient story, applies to all constructed narratives. Lardel explains that the mythic

> actualizes everything it touches: it makes the narrator an actor in his story; the listener, a witness; the world, a present without past or future. The account is made one with what it tells: it is the event itself that is being told, and in being told, is realized. Even in the fairy tale, the expression "once upon a time" does not bring the past as such into the case; it evokes it, in the magical sense of the term, it calls it into being.[12]

This ability of the story to "call the past time into being" is of great value in that first step of reappropriation. It allows the reader a firsthand observation of life in the past. "Firsthand" allows for a right-now-as-it-happens, unfiltered experience of the past; "observation" allows for the proper distance of the reader in order to learn from and appropriate what is observed inside the story in the life outside the fictional re-creation. This ability of the narrative to make its readers present but sufficiently distant at the same time, that is, "in" but not "of" the action, is exactly the kind of situational dynamic needed for stories to have maximum benefit in reappropriation. The present time of the reader mediates the reading process — the reader can assume the position of observer. But the present time of the narrator in the story calls the reader in and describes in detail the full historical context of the moment described in the past — in language, setting, and cultural nuance. Readers see the past and the present *presently* and are thus able, because of the immediacy and freshness of the revelation, to make decisions and appropriate values with greater wisdom and purpose.

3. Composite Artifacts

Because they are also able to incorporate many aspects of life — language, geography, religion, architecture, sociology, politics, popular culture — into one experience, narratives are what we might call "composite artifacts." In addition, then, to their accessible form and their ability to call up the past into the present, narratives offer in their integrated, more lifelike context an opportunity for readers to observe the past with a greater understanding of the interrelationship of setting, behavior, and values. The role of women in church leadership, the largely grassroots effort of building fundraisers, the role of the children and the elderly in traditional black communities, can all be studied independently in separate disciplines. In C. Eric Lincoln's story of an elderly mother of the church, "Mama Lucy," we learn all of those things in their natural, albeit re-created, context.[13]

The "interdisciplinary renderings" of the past allow the dynamics of the full cultural life to be displayed. Separate renderings in sociological analyses, in church or women's histories, economic overviews, or other singular discipline-based accounts of past communities can prevent readers from seeing the interworkings of these aspects in daily life. The composite rendering of life that a story provides brings all these aspects of a culture together to be experienced simultaneously and in context. In so doing, readers or listeners can come to understand how the values and expectations of the culture operated in the lives of individuals on an emotional, psychological, and practical level. "Stories provide a way," says Lynne Tirrell, "of exploring logically and emotionally actions occurring in contexts."[14] These contexts provide a better understanding of the full range of their meaning and provide good examples of how values revealed in the narrative can best be reappropriated in the contemporary period.

4. The Mythos of the Culture

The most important value of imaginative and personal narratives, however, lies in the ability of these narratives to incorporate and employ cultural myths — the sacred, idealized versions of the community's life. The lives of individuals in the segregated communities of the past — if we read only the facts or the journalistic, newsreel version of that past — can easily turn into a long list of negatives of what was denied, abused, or misappropriated. But the lives of the individuals in those communities were governed by something more than these factual negatives. They were governed more consistently by the mythical affirmation of their own individual strength and their unquestioning belief in a certain, divinely inspired deliverance. The mythos of hope, dignity, and deliverance operating in those communities was undaunted by the often brutal realities of the injustice and discrimination. The mythical idea of victory and righteousness was deeply believed in those communities, and it governed how individuals dealt with adversity and how they planned for the future. Their *mythos* of hope and deliverance was not to be shaken by the *logos* that said "hopeless" and "bound."

C. Eric Lincoln's short story "When God Messed over Vernon" is a good example of how in the narrative the writer is able to overlay the negatives of historical circumstance with an idealizing myth.[15] Vernon, an industrious sharecropper who wants during lay-by time to cultivate his own crop and make repairs on his house, is humiliated by white farmers who resent Vernon's industry and are looking for "a good time."[16] When their pranks end in Vernon's retaliating and shooting a planter's son, the farmers burn Vernon's house to the ground with Vernon inside. In the memory of this incident, Vernon's uncle, who is also the narrator, is saddened and disappointed with God for allowing Vernon to meet such a horrible fate. But in recalling the story, he re-members what he has always considered peculiar about the incident: "Funny thing though. They never did find no evidence of po' Vernon in the ashes of that ol' shack. Nothin' a'tall.[17] In not finding Vernon in the ashes, there is the possibility of Vernon's escape, the possibility that he was not "messed over" after all. The uncertainty of his death enshrines the story in the mythic; maybe he has gone away, like the mythical Fly-ing African, in a supernatural moment of transcendence and ultimately won the battle against the mean planters after all. This "funny thing" of not finding the bones, is an element that Lincoln adds to the story. This footnote that the uncle remarkably remembers about the incident is the overlaying of the myth of deliverance and transcendence on what would otherwise be a totally negative experience. With the addition of the mythic, the story of Vernon becomes, in this view, not a story simply about the humiliation of sharecroppers by whites and the share-croppers' powerlessness, but a story about the mystery and certainty of deliverance, a belief that permeated the culture and that the narrative incorporates in a way that an historical accounting of lay-by time and the mistreatment of black sharecroppers would not allow.

The myths of the culture — beliefs that went beyond the logical — such as the one recounted in the story of Vernon, were kept alive in a collective of narratives in segregated black communities. They were taught repeatedly in one-room schoolhouses; spoken humbly in the table blessings; whispered passionately at the beginning of programs; sung, shouted, and cried out about with certainty in churches. There was an ethos of such narratives that pervaded the community, and these narratives provided the strategies for survival.

With the myth of deliverance pervading the culture as it did, it is no wonder that a refrain like "we shall overcome" found resonance among blacks in segregated communities. The essence of their myth was sum-marized in those three words. Their ability to trust in the unseen, to understand the unexplained, to believe that the yet unrealized could happen, kept them forward-looking and full of hope. And it is essen-tially this governing, sustaining, inspiring mythos that those who seek to retrieve the culture of the segregated past want most to reappropriate. They want to have those stories told and believed in the present. They want them seen in context so that a new generation can learn and use the inspiring meanings of those myths in contemporary society.

By being able to extract the mythical values, or what Seymour Katz calls the "essential defining qualities" of the culture — as opposed to every random aspect of its behavior — narratives can shape the experience of the past so as to evoke these qualities, and thus illustrate cultural meaning more clearly and succinctly than can be done by recording every random/objective aspect of the group's behavior. With a knowledge of these deeply embedded myths — the higher, deeper truths of the culture — and by ordering the action in stories to reflect these myths, writers are able to provide, says Katz, "a cognitive model of experience, a hypothetical construction of reality, by means of which we may come to know more about experience than experience alone can show."[18] Experience gives us the everyday reality; myth — the constructed idealized narrative — gives us the explanation of experience that transcends that reality. It is this mythical transcendence of negative historical reality that keeps a group, even a nation, alive and optimistic about the future. "The simple fact," historian William McNeil concludes, "is that communities lived by myths of necessity. For only by acting as if the world made sense can society persist and individuals survive."[19]

Contemporary writers such as novelists Morrison, Wideman, and Lincoln, and personal historians such as Edelman and Taulbert, are aware of the potential of their works to restore and explain the role of myth in traditional black communities, and they are using their works to retell these mythic stories and to educate contemporary readers of myth's transformative potential. Writer Toni Morrison explains that the mythology in these books can provide what the other culture did:

> It provides a transition, a way to see what in fact the dangers are, what are the havens, and what is the shelter. That is true for everybody, but for people who have been culturally parochial for a long time, the novel is the transition. The novel has to provide the richness of the past as well as suggestions of what the use of it is.[20]

For the reader, the myths employed in these stories become the themes, the metaphors, the usable signs they need in contemporary society to survive and triumph. If we extract nothing else from these narratives, we must seek to extract the mythos that these writers incorporate in their stories, and we must try to discover the clues, the lessons, the directives of how to use those myths in the present. This ordering of behavior along the lines and according to the rules of the

"essentials" of a group's culture, improves the quality of the readers' re-
ception of the narrative on a cognitive level — as in *what* we come to
know — and, more importantly, on a cultural level — what *meaning* we
come to give to that behavior.

These contemporary African-American writers offer an entire canon
of such mythological stories. And their narratives can serve, in a similar
way, the metaphorical and referential purpose in the culture for African
Americans today that biblical stories served for earlier generations. As
with the Bible, we can read these stories; we can literally carry these
stories in our hands and access the past and its meaning in the present
again and again. Indeed the survival and moral empowerment of earlier
generations during slavery and segregation — historical moments rife
with horror and injustice — were achieved not from reading journalistic
newspaper reports, social-scientific documentation, or historical tracts,
but from reading and believing mythological stories found in the Bible.
African Americans were drawn to these stories because they were, like
the imaginative stories written by this post-integration generation of
writers, in easily comprehensible narrative form; they were dramatic,
accessible, collective renderings of a people and, in some way, representative of their own lives. But mostly they were appropriated and given
measure in their lives because of the powerful mythological undercur-
rent of these stories. From the opening of the Red Sea to the battle of
Jericho, from David's defeat of Goliath to Daniel's deliverance from the
den of lions, from Genesis to Revelation, the stories of the Bible were
stories that taught African Americans hope — to believe in a way being
available when no way seemed possible. These stories validated a belief in a reality rising not from the logic of historical circumstance but
from the mythos of the possible, from an idea larger than themselves
or their circumstances. And a generation of achievers, the children of
those who lived the myth of those stories, now stands as testimony to
what seemed an irrational belief in deliverance held by their parents.

5. Model for Exemplary Life

By believing in those myths, in calling up the possible, the hopeful, the
triumphant — again and again — in places where, according to historical logic, it should not have been, a generation of African Americans
and their children survived and thrived. And now their life stories,
made exemplary because of their belief in other mythological stories,
serve as the basis for the stories of this post-integration generation of
African-American writers. By appropriating the myths of the Bible in
their own lives, African Americans of earlier generations in turn created, by their own example, new narratives and new myths for their

children to return to, reappropriate, and pass on to the next generation. These stories — memories of the lives of a past generation — must be called into the service of cultural reappropriation, as they are in the works of Marian Wright Edelman and Clifton Taulbert, and as they have been in the autobiographical writings of Benjamin Mays, Pauli Murray, Booker T. Washington, and others. For it is here in the personal narratives that the hoped for, the possible, and the believed are actualized and given voice, and thus made accessible as life examples to others. As Carolyn Heilbrun has so passionately argued,

> We live our lives through texts. They may be read, or chanted, or experienced electronically, or come to us, like the murmuring of our mothers, telling us what convention demands. Whatever their form or medium, stories have formed us all, [and] they are what we must use to make new fictions, new narratives.[21]

Stories call on us, as Heilbrun suggests, not only to learn from the life stories of our ancestors but also to live our lives in ways, as exemplary models, that will allow for the construction of new narratives to be appropriated by future generations. Autobiographies offer the best models for encouraging the continued construction of these exemplary narratives. This exemplary function of the narrative is ultimately the narrative's greatest value. By encouraging a life that makes individuals self-consciously aware of the drama and meaning that their lives should have, narratives can provide, in a manner unlike other forms of presentation, a way to access, interpret, and incorporate on an intellectual and contextual level the ethical values that we want to uncover and examine for their reappropriative potential in the contemporary period.

Implementation and Suggested Texts

One way to implement the use of narratives in our ethical mission is to have classes and seminars that examine the moral and ethical dimensions of these texts. The goals of such classes would be: (1) to discover through cultural analysis of the texts what moral and ethical values are being portrayed, (2) to examine such values within the black church tradition, and (3) to suggest how in different historical contexts these values may be appropriated to achieve ethical leadership in our communities. This course, which might be offered under titles such as "The Black Church Tradition in Literature" or "Ethics and Values in African-American Literature," could include theoretical works in cultural anthropology and ethics and primary readings of works such as those found in the following list of imaginative and autobiographical African-American writers.

Nonfiction

Benjamin Mays, *Born to Rebel*

Marian Wright Edelman, *The Measure of Our Success*

Booker T. Washington, *Up from Slavery*

W. E. B. Du Bois, *Dusk of Dawn*

Pauli Murray, *Proud Shoes*

Maya Angelou, *I Know Why the Caged Bird Sings*

Richard Wright, *Black Boy*

Clifton Taulbert, *Once Upon a Time When We Were Colored*

Chalmers Archer, *Growing Up Black in Rural Mississippi*

William Raspberry, *Looking Back on Us*

Martin Luther King Jr., *Why We Can't Wait*

Howard Thurman, *With Head and Heart: The Autobiography of Howard Thurman*

Karen Fields, *Lemon Swamp and Other Stories*

Charlayne Hunter Gault, *In My Place*

James Comer, *Maggie's American Dream*

Fiction

Toni Morrison, *The Bluest Eye, Sula, Song of Solomon, Tar Baby, Beloved, Jazz*

James Baldwin, *Go Tell It on the Mountain*

John Wideman, *Damballah*

Tina McElroy Ansa, *Baby of the Family*

Alice Walker, *In Love and Trouble, Living by the Word, In Search of Our Mothers' Gardens*

Ernest Gaines, *The Autobiography of Miss Jane Pittman, A Gathering of Old Men, A Lesson before Dying*

C. Eric Lincoln, *The Avenue Clayton City*

Doris Saunders, *Clover*

Paule Marshall, *Praisesong for the Widow*

Notes

1. Pierre Nora, "Between Memory and History: Les Lieux de Memoire," *Representations* 26 (spring 1989): 7.

2. See Clifford Geertz, *The Interpretation of Cultures* (New York: Basic Books, 1973); Ward Goodenough, *Description and Comparison in Cultural Anthropology* (Chicago: Aldine, 1968).

3. Robert Coles, *The Call of Stories: Teaching and the Moral Imagination* (Boston: Houghton Mifflin, 1989).

4. William Bennett, *The Book of Virtues* (New York: Simon and Schuster, 1993).

5. Thomas LeClair, "A Conversation with Toni Morrison: The Language Must Not Sweat," *New Republic*, 21 March 1981, 33–34.

6. Wilfred Samuels, "Going Home: A Conversation with John Edgar Wideman," *Callaloo* 6 (February 1993): 52.

7. Coles, *Call of Stories*, 30.

8. Barbara Hardy, "Towards a Poetics of Fiction: An Approach through Narrative," *Novel* 2 (1968): 5.

9. Louis Mink, "History and Fiction as Modes of Comprehension," *New Literary History* (spring 1970): 557.

10. The "continuous historical present" is the term used to describe the understanding by critics and grammarians that action in fictional narratives is presently occurring while it is being read. In the act of reading, readers activate the story again and again, and always in the time of the story itself. So while the story may be read in, say, 1993, the action of the story, the fictional time in which the reader enters, is always the time re-created in the story. Thus, when readers refer to the action in a fictional narrative, unless the story refers to the action as occurring in the past, they always use the present tense.

11. Walter E. Fluker, "The Ground Has Shifted," sermon delivered at the Harvard Divinity School, Cambridge, Mass., 5 June 1991.

12. Eric Lardel, "The Mythic," in *Sacred Narrative: Readings in the Theory of Myth*, ed. Alan Dundes (Berkeley: University of California Press), 231.

13. C. Eric Lincoln, "Mama Lucy," in *The Avenue Clayton City* (New York: Ballantine, 1988), 151–70.

14. Lynne Tirrell, "Storytelling and Moral Agency," *Journal of Aesthetics and Art Criticism* 48, no. 2 (spring 1990): 117.

15. "When God Messed over Vernon," in C. Eric Lincoln, *Avenue Clayton City* (New York: Ballantine Books, 1989), 151–70.

16. "Lay-by" time refers to a period of two to three weeks in August during which the farmers are waiting for early September to harvest the chopped and weeded cotton. Revivals, quilting bees, reunions, and leisure travel generally occurred during lay-by time. For further discussion, see Pete Daniel, *The Breaking*

of the Land: The Transformation of Corn, Tobacco, and Rice Cultures Since 1880 (Urbana: University of Illinois, 1985).

17. "When God Messed over Vernon," 169.

18. Seymour Katz, " 'Culture' and Literature in American Studies," *American Quarterly* 20 (summer supplement 1968): 323.

19. Cited in Michael Kammen, *Mystic Chords of Memory: The Transformation of Tradition in American Culture* (New York: Knopf, 1991), 25.

20. Charles Raus, *Conversations with American Writers* (New York: Knopf, 1985), 238.

21. Carolyn Heilbrun, *Writing a Woman's Life* (New York: Ballantine, 1988), 37.

7

Ethical Leadership in Black America
Malcolm X, Urban Youth Culture, and the Resurgence of Nationalism
MICHAEL ERIC DYSON

Because Malcolm X, for the duration of his life and most of his death, occupied the shadowy periphery of black cultural politics — subsisting as the suppressed premise of the logic of black bourgeois resistance to racism — his reemergence as a cultural hero is something of a paradox. Malcolm X's newly acclaimed heroism is inseparable from the renaissance of black nationalism, which has as much to do with his revived (and overhauled) heroic status as with his commodification by black and white cultural entrepreneurs. In this essay, I will probe the possibilities for black ethical leadership by examining Malcolm X's black nationalist legacy (and to a lesser extent, Martin Luther King Jr.'s contributions) and relating it to the vibrant black youth culture that has seized upon his life in expressing its visions of cultural survival.

Given this nation's racist legacy, it is no surprise that black folk have at every crucial juncture of their history in America expressed nationalist sentiment.[1] The peculiar social, economic, and political constraints of oppression, stretching from slavery to the present day, have always precipitated varying degrees of resistance, revolt, rebellion, or resentment from African Americans. If nationalism is viewed as an attempt to establish and maintain a nation's identity, growing out of circumstances of cultural conflict and the expression of socially contradictory forces, then black nationalism is even more acutely a response of racial solidarity directed against the premises and practices of white supremacist nationalism.

Black nationalism has usually been viewed as a response to the erosion of communal identity, the eradication of collective self-determination under slavery, and the destructive cultural effects of post-Emancipation rejection of fragile political liberties. Black nationalism was often an expression of healthy self-regard and important self-respect in the midst of an inimical American ethos that had erected a legal structure that reinforced black culture's inferior political status. Unlike other expressions of nationalism, however, black nationalism was coerced into a parasitic relationship to American culture. This confounding irony of black nationalist discourse and practice haunts it to this day.

Black nationalism is often contrasted to liberal integrationist ideology. Liberal integrationism is the belief that the goal of African-American struggles for liberation ought to be the inclusion of blacks in the larger compass of American social, political, and economic privilege, while maintaining a distinct appreciation for African-American culture. In its extreme expression, however, liberal integrationist ideology acquired a bland assimilationist emphasis. Racial assimilationists promote the uncritical adoption by blacks of the norms of civility, education, and culture nurtured in mainstream white American culture. Although overly sharp distinctions between forms of nationalism and integrationism are problematic (the two ideologies often coexist in a figure's thought or at different periods in an institution's or organization's life), the distinctions are helpful in capturing the primary thrusts of belief, goal, and ideology in African-American communities.

The most prominent recent phase of black nationalist activity prior to today's revived movement lasted from 1965 until 1973, from the emergence of Stokely Carmichael as leader of the Black Power movement, until the demise of the Black Panthers. This period saw major black organizations denying white participation in radical civil rights organizations like SNCC, black nationalist leaders advocating armed violence in defense against racist state repression in the form of the police and national guard, the end of the powerful leadership of Malcolm X with his assassination in 1965, the bold articulation of black theology from James Cone in 1969, and the urban rebellion planned and partially implemented by the Black Panthers.

The cultural rebirth of Malcolm X, then, is the remarkable result of complex forces converging to lift him from his violent death in 1965. Malcolm's heroic status hinges largely on the broad, if belated, appeal of his variety of black nationalism to Americans who, when X lived, either ignored or despised him. But Malcolm's appeal is strongest among black youth between the ages of fifteen and twenty-four, who find in X a figure of epic racial achievement.[2] Rap has had a decisive influence in promoting X as a heroic figure. Because of the themes it addresses, and the often militant viewpoints it espouses, rap has often served as the popular cultural elaboration of certain features of X's legacy. Both the obstacles that rap has overcome in establishing itself as a mainstay

of American popular culture — its style of expression (which links it
to a rich black oral culture brilliantly engaged by Malcolm X) — and
its major themes and ideas provide a natural link between X's radical
social vocation and aspects of the cultural agenda of black juvenile culture. Because of the similarity between aspects of hip-hop culture and
Malcolm's public career (for example, charges of violence, the problems
of articulating black rage emanating from the ghetto, and the celebra-
tion of black pride and historical memory), rappers have taken the lead
in asserting X's heroism for contemporary black America.

One of the most obvious and compelling features of rap culture is its
form, which values the spoken word and oral tradition with deep roots
in African-American culture.[3] The oral tradition of African-American
culture is one that X brilliantly participated in, relishing his capacity
to verbally outfox his opponents with a well-placed word or a cleverly
engineered rebuke. His broad familiarity with the devices of African-
American oral culture — the saucy put-down, the feigned agreement
turned to oppositional advantage, the hyperbolic expression generously
employed to make a point, the fetish for powerful metaphor — mark his
public rhetoric.

The hip-hop generation has appropriated X with unequaled passion, pushed along by the same fetish for the word that drove X to
read voraciously and speak with eloquence. X is the rap revolution's
rhetorician of choice, his words forming the ideological framework for
authentic black consciousness. His verbal ferocity has been combined
with the rhythms of James Brown and George Clinton, the three figures
forming a triumvirate of griots dispensing cultural wisdom harnessed to
polyrhythmic beats.

Malcolm's public career, too, is the powerful if perplexing story of
a series of personal and intellectual changes, a constellation of compli-
cated and sometimes conflicting identities, that mark his evolution of
thought and shift in direction. As rapper Michael Franti of the group
The Disposable Heroes of Hiphoprisy says,

> The thing I gained from him is not his symbol as a militant,
> but his ongoing examination of his life and how he was able to
> think critically about himself and grow and change as he en-
> countered new information. That's where I feel that we gain
> strength, through constantly conquering our own shortcomings,
> and questioning our beliefs.[4]

Furthermore, like X's public rallies — which focused black rage on
suitable targets, especially black bourgeois liberal leaders and white
racists — the rap concert encourages the explicit articulation of black

anger in public. And similar to the misconceptions that often prevailed about X's provocative statements about self-defense, perceptions about the automatic or inevitable link between rap and violence are often grounded in ignorance rather than critical investigation of Malcolm's words or deeds.

Because X, too, addressed with unequaled clarity and suasion the predicament of the ghetto poor, he is a natural icon for rap culture. As rappers Ultramagnetic M.C.'s state,

> Everybody still listens to Malcolm X. When he talks you can't walk away. The thing about X is that he attracted and still attracts the people who have given up and live recklessly — the crowd that just don't care what's going on. Making a difference in these people's lives is truly the essence of Malcolm X.[5]

Rappers often point to Malcolm X's phrase, "no sellout, no sellout, no sellout," as the touchstone of a black cultural consciousness intent on preserving the authenticity of black cultural expressions, and as the basis for a true black nationalism.[6] But what precisely about X's black nationalist beliefs is the basis of his revived American heroism, especially for black youth?

First, X's bold and defiant articulation of black rage has won him a new hearing among a generation of black youth whose embattled social status due to an equally resurgent racism makes them sympathetic to X's fiery, often angry, rhetoric. Malcolm's take-no-prisoners approach to racial crisis appeals to young blacks disaffected from white society and alienated from older black generations whose contained style of revolt owes more to Martin Luther King Jr.'s nonviolent philosophy than to X's advocacy of self-defense.

Moreover, Malcolm's articulation of black rage — which, by his own confession, tapped a vulnerability even in Martin Luther King Jr. — has been adopted by participants in the culture of hip-hop, whose rap music often reflects Malcolm's militant posture. These artists, like many of their black peers, find in X's uncompromising rhetoric the confirmation of their instincts about the malignant persistence of American racism. Also, X's ability to say out loud what many blacks could only say privately endeared him to blacks when he was alive, and explains his appeal to youth seeking an explicit articulation of anger at American racism and injustice:

> It was for that undaunted ability to talk back to The Man that so many blacks adored Malcolm, no matter what some thought of his more extremist rhetoric. At a time when most black folks

had to weigh every word they said around white people, Malcolm stood up before crowds and TV cameras and uttered thoughts that most African-Americans gave voice to only in private: that whites would never really accept blacks as equals, and that the promise that blacks could get ahead if only they acted "more white" was a cruel illusion. Even more gratifying, Malcolm told off the white man with an eloquence, wit and confidence that was a match for any white orator.[7]

The second element of X's nationalism that has cemented his heroic status is his withering indictments of the limitations of black bourgeois liberalism, expressed most clearly in the civil rights protest against white racial dominance. X showed little tolerance for the strategies, tactics, and philosophy of nonviolence that were central to the civil rights movement led by Martin Luther King Jr.[8] Further, King's limited successes in reaching those most severely punished by poverty only reinforced the value of X's criticism of civil rights ideology.

If some young blacks now consider Malcolm X more of a hero than Martin Luther King, it's a testimony to both the success and the failure of King's dream. King's crusade for legal equality and greater opportunity has made life better for millions of blacks, allowing them to get better jobs, move to the suburbs....But that exodus has had the cruel effect of making those left behind — the kind of poor urban blacks who grew up like Malcolm — even worse off.[9]

X's pointed denunciations of black liberal protest against white racism hinged on the belief that black people should maintain independence from the very people who had helped oppress them, namely, white people. Black bourgeois liberal protest incorporated white cooperation in the struggle to secure the fragile gains that civil rights groups aimed at in their quest for social justice. As one rap group explains of Malcolm's appeal, "The reason why Malcolm X has an influence on today's youth is because his influence as a leader was certainly equal, if not better than Dr. Martin Luther King. Everybody still listens to Malcolm X."[10] Another rap group believes that the "legacy of Malcolm X is to provide a clear counterpoint to the nonviolent/passive resistance theme presented by Dr. Martin Luther King, Jr."[11] X's heroic appeal as a critic of black bourgeois protest of white racism is summarized by C. Eric Lincoln, who contends that the source of Malcolm's undying magnetism lies in the simple fact that we have not yet overcome.... For many of the kids in the ghetto, we are right back where we were. The few advances that have been made have not reached them. So if we didn't make it with King, what have we to lose? We might as well make it with Malcolm.[12]

The third element of X's black nationalist ideology was his advocacy of an alternative black spirituality and religious cosmos that provided bold relief to the ethic of love advocated in black Christian conceptions of social protest. Though this element is linked to Malcolm's denunciation of black liberal protest philosophies and strategies, X's alternative black spirituality was rooted in the religious worldview of the Nation of Islam and promoted a black public theodicy that demonized whites and white racism as unquestionably evil.[13] Though X's understanding of white racism was rooted in a theological narrative that ascribed religious significance to the inequitable relationship between whites and blacks, his colorful articulation of his beliefs in his public addresses forged the expression of a black public theodicy with which even secular or non-Muslim blacks could identify.[14]

The central element of Malcolm's alternative black spirituality was its rejection of the belief that black people should redeem white people through black bloodshed, sacrifice, and suffering. "We don't believe that Afro-Americans should be victims any longer," X said. "We believe that bloodshed is a two-way street."[15] He also contended that not "a single white person in America would sit idly by and let someone do to him what we black men have been letting others do to us."[16] X's theological premises forced him to the conclusion that white violence must be met with intelligent opposition and committed resistance, even if potentially violent means must be adopted in self-defense against white racism. Carlos Cubas illumines Malcolm's black public theodicy while explaining his heroic appeal to a contemporary African-American juvenile culture:

> To all Black Muslims, white men were "blue-eyed devils" who had brainwashed the so-called "Negro" into thinking that he had no history, no value, no self-worth. It became easy for Black Muslims to focus themselves on exposing the American myth of white supremacy and more importantly to work amongst themselves to achieve self-determination and the "true" freedom granted all Negroes by the Emancipation Proclamation. If Elijah was the Prophet of a black god, then Malcolm X was to be his avenging angel.[17]

Though X would, near the end of his life, alter his views and admit the humanity of whites and their potential for assistance, he maintained a strong philosophical commitment to proclaiming the evil of white racism and to detailing its lethal consequences in poor black communities.

The fourth element of X's black nationalism — and indeed a large part of the cultural crisis that has precipitated Malcolm's mythic return — is rooted in a characteristic quest in black America: the search for a secure and empowering racial identity. That quest is perennially frustrated by the demands of our culture to cleanse ethnic and racial particularity at the altar of a superior American identity, substituting the terms of one strain of nationalism for the priorities of another. By this common ritual of national identity, for instance, the Irish, Poles, Italians, and Jews have been absorbed into a universal image of common citizenship. But the transformation of black cultural identity is often poorly served by this process, impeded as much by the external pressures of racism and class prejudice as by internal racial resistance to an "inclusion" that would rob blacks of whatever power and privilege they already enjoy in their own domains.

As further testimony to the contemporary black quest for a secure racial identity, gusts of racial pride sweep across black America as scholars retrieve the lost treasures of an unjustly degraded African past. This quest continues a project of racial reclamation begun in earnest in the sixties but recast to fit the needs of end-of-the-century utopian nationalists (ranging from followers of Leonard Jeffries to what Huey Newton termed "pork-chop nationalists"). The Afrocentric movement has quickened the debate about multicultural education and cast a searching light upon the intellectual blindness and racist claims of Eurocentric scholars, even as it avoids acknowledging the romantic features of its own household.

Malcolm's unabashed love for black history, his relentless pedagogy of racial redemption through cultural consciousness and racial self-awareness, mesh effortlessly with black Americans' (especially black youth's) recovery of their African roots. As rapper KRS-One summarized a crucial feature of X's legacy, black children will "come to know that they come from a long race and line of kings, queens, and warriors," a knowledge that will make them "have a better feeling of themselves."[18]

The final aspect of Malcolm's black nationalism that has made him a hero is his unfettered championing of the politics of black masculinity. Few other aspects of Malcolm's rejuvenated appeal have been as prominently invoked as Malcolm's focus on the plight and place of black men in American society. In light of the contemporary cultural status of black men, particularly young black males, it is easy to comprehend X's heroic status as a defender of black men.

The difficult personal and social conditions of most young black males make Malcolm's rhetoric about the obstacles to true black manhood and the virtues of a strong black masculinity doubly attractive. Indeed, blacks from the very beginning of Malcolm's career have accented his focus on a virile black manhood denied them because of white racism as a primary contribution of his vocation.

> Asked to sum up what Malcolm and his message represented to them, blacks through the decades have come back to one word: "manhood." In the beautiful eulogy that actor Ossie Davis gave at Malcolm's funeral . . . he proclaims, "Malcolm was our manhood! This was his meaning to his people." It was how Malcolm himself used to taunt white people: "I am the man you think you are." In an age when white men wanted to be John Wayne or Steve McQueen, Malcolm offered an image of a black gunslinger to his people — a man who was gentle and upright with family and friends but fearless toward adversaries.[19]

From gang members to preachers, from college students to black intellectuals, Malcolm's focus on black men has made him a critical spokesman for black males denied the fundamental right to exist without the sexual jealousy and social fear that haunt unjustly aggrieved black men.

But if the reemergence of black nationalism and Malcolm's explosive popularity go hand in hand — are mirror images of response to the continuing plague of an equally rejuvenated racism — then their limitations, as well as their strengths, are revealing. In this regard, two aspects of Malcolm's legacy are striking: the troubling consequences of his focus on the black male predicament, and the ironic (and unintended) uses of black nationalist discourse by a black middle class often closed off from nationalism's most desperate constituency — the black ghetto poor.

Malcolm's brand of black nationalism was not only a fierce attack on white Americans, but also a sharp rebuke to black women. A product of his times, Malcolm went to extremes in demonizing women, saying that the "closest thing to a woman is a devil." Although he later revised his beliefs, confessing his regret at "spit[ting] acid at the sisters" and contending that they should be treated equally, Malcolm's contemporary black nationalist heirs have failed to take his changed position on gender seriously. Though X, as Patricia Hill Collins notes, died "before Black feminist politics were articulated in the 1970s and 1980s," his

Black nationalism projects an implicit and highly problematic gender analysis. Given today's understanding of the gender-specific structures of Black oppression...his ideas about gender may be interpreted in ways detrimental not only to both African-American women and men but to policies of Black community development....Malcolm X's treatment of gender reflected the widespread belief of his time that, like race, men's and women's roles were "natural" and were rooted in biological difference.[20]

Like the early Malcolm and other sixties nationalists, contemporary black nationalists have cast the pursuit of racial liberation in terms of a quest for masculine self-realization. Such a strategy not only borrows ideological capital from the white patriarchy that has historically demeaned black America, but it blunts awareness of how the practice of patriarchy by black men has created another class of victims within black communities.

Further, the strategy of viewing racial oppression exclusively through a male lens distorts the suffering of black women at the hands of white society and blurs the focus on the especially difficult choices that befall black women caught in a sometimes bewildering nexus of kinship groups assembled around race, class, and gender. Reducing black suffering to its lowest common male denominator not only presumes a hierarchy of pain that removes priority from black female struggle, but also trivializes the analysis and actions of black women in the realization of black liberation. Given Malcolm's mature pronouncements, his heirs have reneged upon the virtues of his enlightened gender beliefs.

The cultural renaissance of Malcolm X also embodies the paradoxical nature of black nationalist politics over the past two decades: those most aided by its successes have rarely stuck around to witness the misery of those most hurt by its failures. The truth is that black nationalist rhetoric has helped an expanding black middle class gain increased material comfort while black nationalism's most desperate constituency — the working class and working poor — continue to toil in the aftermath of nationalism's unrealized political promise.

Ironically, talk of black cultural solidarity and racial loyalty have propelled the careers of intellectuals, cultural artists, and politicians as they seek access to institutions of power and ranks of privilege, even within black communities, as esteemed vox populi. The trouble is that they are often cut off from the very people on whose behalf they ostensibly speak, the perks and rewards of success insulating them from the misery of their constituencies.

The greatest irony of contemporary black nationalism may be its use by members of the black middle class to consolidate their class interests *at the expense* of working and poor blacks. By refusing to take class seriously — or only halfheartedly as they decry, without irony, the moves of a self-serving black bourgeoisie! — many nationalists discard an analytical tool crucial for exploring the causes of black racial and economic suffering. If X's brand of black nationalism is to have an even more substantive impact on contemporary racial politics, his heirs must relentlessly criticize his limitations while celebrating his heroic embrace of issues long denied currency in mainstream social discourse.

This is not to say that nationalism's vaunted alternative, bourgeois liberal integrationism, has enjoyed wide success, either, in bringing the black masses within striking distance of prosperity, or at least to parity with white middle and working classes. Commentators usually gloss over this fact when comparing the legacies of Malcolm X and Martin Luther King Jr. For the most part, Malcolm and Martin have come to symbolize the parting of paths in black America over the best answer to racial domination. While Malcolm's strident rhetoric is keyed in by nationalists at the appropriate moments of black disgust with the pace and point of integration, King's conciliatory gestures are evoked by integrationists as the standard of striving for the promised land of racial harmony and economic equity.

In truth, however, King's admirers have also forsaken the bitter lessons of his mature career in deference to the soaring optimism of his dream years.[21] King discerned as early as 1965 that the fundamental problems of black America were economic in nature, and that a shift in strategies was necessary for the civil rights movement to become a movement for economic equality. After witnessing wasted human capital in the slums of Watts and Chicago, and after touring the rural wreckage of life in Mississippi's deep Delta, King became convinced that the only solution to black suffering was to understand it in relation to a capitalist economy that hurt all poor people. He determined that nothing short of a wholesale criticism and overhaul of existing economic arrangements could effectively remedy the predicament of the black poor and working class.

This is a far cry from contemporary black capitalist and business strategies that attempt to address the economic plight of black Americans by creating more black millionaires. Highly paid entertainers and athletes participate in the lucrative culture of consumption by selling their talents to the highest bidder in the marketplace — a legacy, we are often reminded, of King's and the civil rights movement's vision of a just society where social goods are distributed according to merit, not color. King's willingness, toward the end of his life, to question the legitimacy of the present economic order and to challenge the logic of capital has been obscured by appeals to his early beliefs about the virtues of integration.

The relative failure of both black nationalist and integrationist strategies to affect large numbers of black Americans beyond the middle and upper class raises questions about how progressive ethical leadership can emerge by employing and expanding Malcolm's and Martin's legacies to address the present crises in black America. Black progressive intellectuals and activists must view class, gender, and sexual preference as crucial components of a complex and sophisticated explanation of the problems of black America. There are at least two advantages to such an approach. First, it provides a larger range of social and cultural variables from which to choose in depicting the vast array of forces that constrain black economic, political, and social progress. Second, it acknowledges the radical diversity of experiences within the black communities, offering a more realistic possibility of addressing the particular needs of a wide range of blacks: the ghetto poor, gays and lesbians, single black females, working mothers, underemployed black men, and elderly blacks, for instance.

Black progressives must also deepen Malcolm's and Martin's criticisms of capitalism and their leanings toward radical democracy. The prevailing economic policies have contributed to the persistent poverty of the poorest Americans (including great numbers of blacks), and the relative inability of most Americans to reap the real rewards of political democracy and economic empowerment. A radical democratic perspective raises questions about the accountability of the disproportionately wealthy, providing a critical platform for criticizing black capitalist and business strategies that merely replicate unjust economic practices.

A radical democratic perspective — which criticizes capital accumulation and the maximization of profit for the few without regard to its effects on the many, which advocates an equitable redistribution of wealth through progressive taxation and the increased financial responsibility of the truly wealthy, and which promotes the restructuring of social opportunities for the neediest through public policy and direct political intervention — also encourages the adoption of political and social policies that benefit all Americans, while addressing the specific needs of blacks, such as universal health care. Presently, black Americans are overwhelmingly represented among the thirty-seven million uninsured in our nation. A radical democratic perspective asks why a nation that pays over $820 billion, or 13 percent of the GNP, for the well-insured cannot redistribute its wealth through a progressive tax of the wealthiest 2 percent (and a fair tax on the top 50 percent) of our country to help provide the additional $50–60 billion needed to provide universal health coverage. By refusing to take class seriously, many black nationalists discard an analytical tool crucial for understanding black racial and economic suffering.

The quest for black racial and economic justice has been heavily influenced by black religious conceptions of justice, charity, equality, and freedom. During the civil rights movement, King articulated black Christian conceptions of justice through the language of human rights and the political language of civil religion. Likewise, Malcolm X expressed his conceptions of divine retribution for racial injustice and the religious basis for healthy black self-esteem through black Islamic and, subsequently, orthodox Islamic belief that accorded with black secular ideas about racial self-determination and cultural pride. A radical democratic perspective encourages the broad expression of concepts of justice, equality, and political freedom that are tempered by regard for the widest possible audience of intellectual interlocutors and political participants, including those trained in the rich traditions of black social protest.

Finally, black progressives must make sensible but forceful criticisms of narrow visions of black racial identity, especially after the debacle involving Clarence Thomas and Anita Hill. That wrenching drama provided a glimpse of the underdeveloped state of gender analysis in most black communities and provoked a serious reconsideration of the politics of racial unity and loyalty. In reflecting on Clarence Thomas's nomination to the Supreme Court, black Americans were torn between fidelity to principles of fairness and justice, agonizing over his qualifications for office, and troubling over whether blacks should support one of their own despite his opposition to many of the legal principles cherished by black communities.

The introduction of Anita Hill's perspective into this already complex calculus ripped open ancient antagonisms between black women and men. In a public and painful manner, the hearings forced many black Americans to a new awareness of the need to place principles of justice above automatic appeals to racial loyalty premised exclusively on skin color. Many Americans, including many blacks, came to a clearer understanding of the social construction of racial identity, recognizing that black folk are by no means a homogeneous group. The differences that factors such as geography, sexual preference, gender, and class make in the lives of black Americans are too complex to be captured in a monolithic model of racial unity. Progressive blacks share more ideological and political ground with a white progressive such as

Barbara Ehrenreich, for instance, than they do with conservatives such as Clarence Thomas or even Anita Hill.

For black leaders, the political and social significance of this fact should be the building of bridges across the chasm of color in the common embrace of ideals that transcend racial rooting. Progressive blacks must join with progressive Latinas and Latinos, gays and lesbians, feminists, environmental activists, and all others who profess and practice personal and social equality and democracy. The relative absence of sustained progressive black political opposition, or even a radical political organization that expresses the views of the working class and working poor, signals a loss of the political courage and nerve in the United States that characterized Malcolm and Martin at their best.

In the end, Malcolm and Martin are in varying degrees captives of their true believers, trapped by literal interpreters who refuse to let them, in Malcolm's words, "turn the corner." The bulk of each man's achievements lay in his willingness to place truth over habit in the quest for the best route to social reconstruction and racial redemption. Their legacy to us is the imagination and energy to pursue the goals of liberation upon as wide a scale as the complexities of our contemporary crises demand and our talents allow.

Notes

1. For insightful treatments of black nationalism, see John Bracey Jr., August Meier, and Elliot Rudwick, eds., *Black Nationalism in America* (Indianapolis: Bobbs-Merrill, 1970); Wilson Jeremiah Moses, *The Golden Age of Black Nationalism: 1950–1925* (Hamden, Conn.: Archon Books, 1978); and Alphonso Pinkney, *Red, Black, and Green: Black Nationalism in the United States* (London: Cambridge University Press, 1976).

2. "Malcolm X," *Newsweek*, 16 November 1992, 72.

3. See Lawrence Levine, *Black Culture and Black Consciousness: Afro-American Folk Thought from Slavery to Freedom* (New York: Oxford University Press, 1977).

4. "A Tribute to Malcolm X," *Black Beat*, 1992, 15.

5. "Tribute to Malcolm X," 13.

6. "Tribute to Malcolm X," 48.

7. "Malcolm X," 70.

8. I am not suggesting here that King was the civil rights movement or that his accomplishments exclusively define its scope of achievements. I am suggesting that he is the most powerful symbol of the movement, however, and as a result was often the most visible target of X's attacks on its strategies, goals, and methods.

9. "Malcolm X," 71.

10. "Tribute to Malcolm X," 13.

11. "Tribute to Malcolm X," 12.

12. "Malcolm X," 71–72.

13. See C. Eric Lincoln, *The Black Muslims in America*, rev. ed. (Boston: Beacon Press, 1973).

14. "Tribute to Malcolm X," 70.

15. "Tribute to Malcolm X," 50.

16. "Tribute to Malcolm X," 49.

17. "Tribute to Malcolm X," 7–8.

18. "Tribute to Malcolm X," 12.

19. "Malcolm X," 70.

20. Patricia Hill Collins, "Learning to Think for Ourselves: Malcolm X's Black Nationalism Reconsidered," in *Malcolm X: In Our Own Image*, ed. Joe Wood (New York: St. Martin's Press, 1992), 62, 78.

21. For further comment on this aspect of King's legacy, see my op-ed, "King's Light, Malcolm's Shadow," *New York Times*, 18 January 1993, 19.

Index